Robert Van Bergen

The Story Of Japan

1897

Robert Van Bergen

The Story Of Japan
1897

ISBN/EAN: 9783744640428

Printed in Europe, USA, Canada, Australia, Japan

Cover: Foto ©ninafisch / pixelio.de

More available books at **www.hansebooks.com**

The Story of Japan

Table of Contents

- The Story of Japan
- About Pyrrhus Press
- HOW JIMMU WAS MADE THE FIRST EMPEROR OF JAPAN
- THE STORY OF YAMATO DAKÉ
- PRINCE BRAVEST'S CONQUESTS
- THE FIRST INVASION OF KOREA
- BUDDHISM BROUGHT TO JAPAN
- THE OLDEST CLANS OF JAPAN
- MINAMOTO DEFEATS TAIRA
- THE STORY OF 'YOUNG OX'
- THE LAST OF THE MINAMOTO
- AN INDEPENDENT TENNÔ
- CHRISTIANITY IN JAPAN
- A GREAT GENERAL
- THE LORD OF THE GOLDEN WATER GOURDS
- SECOND INVASION OF KOREA
- THE THREE HOLLYHOCK LEAVES
- THE DUTCH IN JAPAN
- PERSECUTIONS OF THE CHRISTIANS
- RESTRICTIONS OF THE DUTCH
- A VISIT TO THE REGENT
- A SHREWD JUDGE
- TOSA'S REVENGE
- A WIFE'S NOBLE ACT
- THE FORTY-SEVEN RÔNIN
- VARIOUS ATTEMPTS TO TRADE WITH JAPAN
- A RUSSIAN CAPTIVE
- ENGLISH ATTEMPTS TO TRADE WITH JAPAN
- THE UNITED STATES SEEKS TRADE WITH JAPAN
- HOW PERRY SECURED A TREATY
- JAPAN IN PERRY'S TIME
- JAPAN OPENED
- THE TOKUGAWA REGENTS STEP OUT

- HOW A SAMURAI COMMITTED HARA-KIRI
- THE TENNÔ LEAVES HIS SECLUSION
- SAIGO TAKAMORI
- JAPAN'S PROGRESS
- WAR WITH CHINA
- MUTSUHITO, EMPEROR OF JAPAN

The Story of Japan

R. Van Bergen

About Pyrrhus Press

Pyrrhus Press specializes in bringing books long out of date back to life, allowing today's readers access to yesterday's treasures.

This is a history of Japan that traces the founding legends of the nation that date back centuries.

HOW JIMMU WAS MADE THE FIRST EMPEROR OF JAPAN

LONG, long ago, only a short time after the heavens had been separated from the earth, the sun goddess looked down and saw that wicked people did much as they pleased. Now she was one of those women who liked to have order everywhere. So she made her son Ninigi (nee-nee-gee) a human being, sent him down to found a new race, and ordered him to see that his children and children's children should rule justly over the land she gave them,—and that land was Japan.

Before Ninigi went down to the earth, his mother gave him three presents. The first was a mirror, which was an emblem of her own soul; the second was a sword made by the gods themselves, so sharp that it could cut through almost anything; and the third was a fine ball of crystal.

So Ninigi came down and began his work. Of course, he had a good deal of trouble with his neighbors, who had not invited him and did not want him. But he knew that his mother was a goddess, and that therefore he had a right to rule over them. So whether they liked it or not, he made himself king and punished them severely when they did not mind him.

After he had restored order, he married and settled down. He had several children, the oldest of whom was named Prince Light-the-Fire, and the youngest Prince Put-the-Fire-Out. Light-the-Fire was very fond of fishing, and his youngest brother became a great hunter. But one day Prince Light-the-Fire thought he would like to go hunting; so he asked his brother to give him his bow and arrow, and promised in return to lend him his hook and line. Prince Put-the-Fire-Out agreed to this and went fishing, but unluckily he broke the line and lost the hook. He did not think it a serious mishap, and when he reached home, told his brother that he would give him a thousand fishhooks for the one he had lost. But Prince Light-the-Fire was very angry, and scolded so much that Prince Put-the-Fire-Out went to the seashore to escape his brother's wrath, and at the same time to think of what he should do.

He was sitting on the beach, when he heard footsteps behind him, and, turning round, saw a little weazen-faced old fellow, who asked him what he was doing there. Put-the-Fire-Out at once thought this must be some god who might give him good advice, so he told him what had happened. The old fellow, who was indeed one of the gods, took a fancy to the young prince. He told him that the best thing to do was to go to the sea god's palace, and gave him directions to enable him to find his way. "You will know the palace when you see it," said he, "for it is, built of fish scales; in front of the gate is a well, and near the well, a cassia tree. When you get there, you must climb the tree, and wait to see what happens."

"Anything is better than to go back to my brother without his hook," thought Prince Put-the-Fire-Out; so he built a boat, and sailed to the Under-the-Ground-Far-Away country, where the sea god lived. At last he saw the palace, and after hiding his boat, climbed the tree. He had not been there very long when a princess, daughter of the sea god, came to the well with a pitcher. She may have seen Prince Put-the-Fire-Out while he was climbing, or she may have expected him. At any rate, she was not at all frightened, but offered him a drink of water. While she was drawing it, he took a jewel from his necklace and hid it in his mouth. She handed him the water and while he pretended to drink, he dropped the jewel into the pitcher. The princess saw it, and was so pleased that she invited him to come into the palace.

She was pretty, and, of course, the prince married her. For three years he lived happily, and not even once did he think of his brother. But one day, quite suddenly, he remembered the lost fishhook, and thought of his brother's anger, and without knowing it, he sighed deeply. His friends, noticing his grief, questioned him as to the cause, and thereupon he told his tale. When he had finished, the old sea god ordered all the fish to appear, and soon the hook was found in the throat of one of them, whence it was extracted with some difficulty.

Prince Put-the-Fire-Out now wanted to go home on a visit and take the hook to his brother. His wife and his father-in-law had no objection, and the latter gave him as a farewell gift two jewels, telling him that if he drew out the first the water would rise higher and higher until he put it away; and if he held out the other, the water would run out until the sea itself was dry. With these two jewels, and a great many kind wishes from the people of the sea god, the prince returned to his home.

Prince Light-the-Fire was not at all pleased when he saw Put-the-Fire-Out return, and did not seem to care even for the old fishhook. To rid himself of his brother, he tried to kill him; but Prince Put-the-Fire-Out showed the flood jewel, and the water rose until Light-the-Fire was in danger of being drowned. Then he said he was very sorry that he had treated his younger brother so badly. "Call off the water." he cried, "and I will induce our father to make you his heir."

Prince Put-the-Fire-Out agreed to this. He showed the other jewel until the water had gone down to the proper level, and his brother was saved.

So Prince Put-the-Fire-Out succeeded Ninigi. He reigned five hundred years, and his son was the father of Jimmu, the first emperor of Japan.

Now, although this story sounds like a fairy tale, most Japanese children and even many grown people believe it to be true. This is why they call their country Nippon (nee-pon), which means Sunrise Land, and their emperor Tennô (ten-noh), that is, Heaven Child, or Tenshi Sama (ten-shee sah-mah), which means Lord Heaven. And in many of their churches or temples they have a mirror, a sword, and a crystal ball, to remind them of the presents given by the sun goddess to the ancestor of the Tennô. They look upon their emperor as a god, and a Japanese would be punished quite severely if he should pass before a mirror in a temple, and not bow low before it. If you should go to Japan, you would not be expected to do this; but you would have to be careful not to talk lightly of the Japanese beliefs, for these people are very proud of having an emperor who is descended from the sun goddess.

THE STORY OF YAMATO DAKÉ

EMPEROR JIMMU (jim-moo) had been dead a long time, and ten other Tennôs had also been buried, when the Bravest of Warriors was born. He was the son of the twelfth Tennô, and was very handsome. Besides this, he was brave and quick-witted, so that his father had great confidence in him. When still a young man, he was ordered by the emperor to go to the island of Kiushiu (kyoo-shoo) to punish some people who had raised a rebellion. Before he went on board the ship that was to carry him across, his aunt, who was a priestess and very fond of her handsome nephew, gave him a queer-looking package, and told him not to open it until he was close to the rebel camp.

The young prince set sail, and arrived safe and sound in Kiushiu. He lost no time in starting for the place where the rebels were said to have their camp. He did not take many armed men with him; for he intended to pick a quarrel with the rebel chief and kill him. He knew that the rebels would submit as soon as their leader was slain. When he reached the mountains where they had their camp, he saw that it would be almost impossible to attack them, so strong was their position, and he did not know what to do.

As he was thinking about it, making many plans, which he rejected on account of the risk their fulfillment would involve, his eye fell upon his aunt's mysterious package. "Surely," he thought, "I am now close enough to the rebel camp to open it. Perhaps this gift will help me." So he carefully untied the package, and found therein a girl's dress.

At first the prince did not know what to make of it, and perhaps he thought that his aunt had chosen an odd time to play a joke on him. But after a while he was struck with an idea, and the more he considered it, the better he liked it. So he laughed out heartily, and then, stretching himself under a tree, fell asleep.

The next morning he called his trusty followers, and informed them that he would be absent for a few days; he told them what to do and where to hide, that they might be within call, and march upon the camp at a given signal. When he was satisfied that his orders were fully understood, he plunged into the forest, carrying his sword and the girl's dress provided by his aunt. As soon as he was alone, he put on the dress, and hid his own clothes. When he looked into a brook, he saw a handsome girl, instead of the young warrior who had entered the glade. He chuckled as he saw himself so transformed, and, hiding his sword under his clothes assumed a girlish gait and walked slowly in the direction of the rebel camp.

The first day he did not meet anybody; and he was rather glad, for it gave him time to practice a girl's ways and manners. The next morning, however, he met some men; and from the respect paid to one of them, he knew that he must be the rebel chief. The young prince's heart began to beat fast; and had his enemy been alone, he would have slain him at once. The chief came smilingly to meet the pretty girl and asked who she was and where she lived, but for, answer he received only blushes and smiles. Nevertheless the chief was well pleased when, after much coaxing, the girl accepted an invitation to attend a banquet to be given the next day in his cave.

The next day, the prince again put on the girl's dress, and he made up his mind that the time had come to kill the chief, and so put an end to the rebellion. As he went on, thinking how he might lead to a quarrel, he did not forget to assume the shy airs of a girl. When the chief saw him coming through the forest, he went to meet his guest, and leading him into the cave, invited him to sit beside him. When the banquet was at its height, the men grew quarrelsome and at last came to blows. This was what the prince had hoped for, and when the rebel chief arose to restore order, the prince drew his sword, and with one blow severed the chief's head from his body. In the confusion that followed, he gained the entrance to the cave, and gave the signal to his band. In a few moments the cave was surrounded and the rebels were captured. The men outside the cave, deprived of their leader, laid down their arms, and the rebellion was at an end.

For this daring deed the prince was named Yamato Daké (yah-mah-toh dah-kay), or the Bravest of the Brave. We shall call him Bravest, which is shorter and means almost the same thing. For this prince had several other adventures which must be told here.

After his return home, his father, the emperor, who was now a very old man,—a hundred and twenty years old, the Japanese books tell us,—was very much vexed because the people living to the east of his dominions would not become subject to him. So he asked Prince Bravest to take an army and conquer them. The prince gladly obeyed, and as the warriors all loved and trusted him, he had no difficulty in raising troops. Before taking leave of his father, he went to bid good-by to his aunt. She made him a present of a wonderful sword called Cloud Cluster, because it had been taken in the clouds, from the tail of an eight-headed dragon that had been killed by one of the prince's many divine ancestors. Besides this, she gave him a small bag, and told him not to open it except when in extreme danger. Prince Bravest thanked her, and after taking a respectful leave of his aged father, placed himself at the head of his army and marched away. His wife had begged him so hard to let her go with him that at the last moment he consented.

You have all heard or read in your geography of beautiful Fuji Yama (foo-jee yah-mah) or Fuji Mountain, a high extinct volcano, standing out snow-clad against the deep blue sky. The Japanese delight in painting it, and on many a picture brought from that far-away land you will see a mountain resembling white old Fuji. It was in the plain at the foot of this mountain that the enemy had made a stand. Their spies had told them of the march of the Bravest, and as they preferred remaining independent even to being governed by an emperor whose ancestor was a goddess, there was nothing to do but to fight for it.

Prince Bravest went into camp, happy in the prospect of a battle, although the enemy greatly outnumbered his army. In the morning he was awakened by the smell of smoke, and when daylight appeared he saw that the enemy had set fire to the long grass and bush of the plain. The situation of his army was now one of grave peril, and he thought of his aunt's bag.

When he opened it, he found a flint and steel. This gave him an idea. Seizing his sword, he began to mow down the grass and bushes around the camp—an example that was speedily followed by his warriors. As soon as a sufficient space had been cleared, he made a counter fire, so that his army escaped without the loss of a man. When the fire was burnt out, and the smoke had cleared away, the enemy expected to find the burnt corpses of their invaders. But when they saw that the army of the Bravest had remained unscathed, they ascribed this miracle to the intervention of the divine ancestors, and hastened to make peace by submitting to the emperor.

PRINCE BRAVEST'S CONQUESTS

THERE are a great many Americans who visit Japan, for it is a beautiful country. Many of them land in Yokohama (yoh-koh-hah-mah), because that city is nearest to the Pacific coast. All the land around is a great plain, with here and there a hill. But if one goes by railroad toward the west, a few hours' ride will bring one to Odawara (oh-dah-wah-rah), at the foot of the Hakone (hah-koh-nay) range. In the summer, when it is very hot in the plain, most of the foreigners in Japan, and a great many Japanese as well, go to one of the many resorts in these mountains, where the scenery is so lovely that every one who has been there longs to go again. On the top of the mountains is a fine lake named Hakone. It is quite large, and is supposed to be the crater of one of the extinct volcanoes, of which there are a great many in Japan.

Prince Bravest led his army over the Hakone Mountains, and entered the great plain at its eastern base. As he marched on, he came to a broad river emptying into the ocean close by; but now the god of the sea raised such a tempest that it was impossible to cross. Prince Bravest at first thought it was an ordinary storm; but when several days passed and the tempest did not abate, he suspected that it had been sent by one of the gods. He therefore ordered the priests to find out the cause of this unlucky weather, and they very soon told him that it was sent by the sea god, who thought himself abused by the army of the Bravest; and that his wrath could be appeased only by some person volunteering to drown himself.

Here was a difficulty. There was not a warrior in the prince's army who would not gladly have risked his life in battle, even with a most powerful enemy; and every man was ready to die by his own sword, if such a sacrifice should be necessary. But to die by drowning is so inglorious that the warriors looked at each other in silence, but not one volunteered.

While the army was waiting and the prince was considering how he might overcome this unexpected difficulty, his wife could not help noticing that he was worried, and she soon found out the cause. She loved her husband and her country so dearly that she quickly decided to sacrifice herself. Quietly she set about making her preparations, and when she had arranged all her affairs, she went to the river, leaped in, and was drowned.

The prince, deeply shocked at his wife's heroic death, did not notice the waters subsiding as a sign that the sea god's wrath had been appeased; and he remained on the bank of the river, bewailing her loss. After seven days the comb which she had been wearing in her hair was washed ashore. By this time the prince was firmly convinced of his wife's death, and he gave orders to break up the camp. He kept the comb as a precious relic of his wife's love and devotion.

Prince Bravest crossed the river that had caused him so much wretchedness, and tried to forget his loss by pursuing the conquest with more zeal than ever. Sometimes one god would help him and speed him on his way, and at other times he would be worried and opposed by another. But he succeeded in his work, although it was three years before the eastern people would recognize the emperor as their master. When he turned homeward, he took a road more to the north than the one by which he had come. His army, on the march, reached a point from which they could see the unlucky river, and even the place where the prince had lost his wife. When the prince looked upon this spot, he said with a deep sigh, "Adzuma!" (ad-zoo-mah), which means, "My wife!" And so even to this day, Japanese poets speak of eastern Japan as Adzuma.

Some time ago, the Japanese government bought a man-of-war, the Stonewall, from the United States. When this vessel arrived in Japan, its name was changed to Adzuma.

Prince Bravest returned home, but he did not live long. He was changed, we are told, into a great white bird and flew to heaven.

This is the story as it is told in Japanese books, and thus the children learn it as part of the history of their country. The truth is that in the beginning the emperor reigned over only a small part of Japan. He conquered Kiushiu and a part of the center of Hondo. Afterwards he extended these conquests until the south of Hondo belonged to him. Yamato was the name first given to Japan. It will be well to remember this, for when I am telling you of the famous men of to-day, you will hear much of the Spirit of Old Japan, and the daring deeds it has inspired.

THE FIRST INVASION OF KOREA

THE most famous empress of Japan was named Jingu (jin-goo). In her reign the Japanese were so strong that they began to look for other countries to conquer, and Empress Jingu thought Korea (koh-ree-ah) would be the easiest to take.

If you look on the map, you will see to the west of Japan, and not far distant from the island of Kiushiu, a peninsula. On our maps it is called Korea, but the people who live in it have named it "Land of the Morning Calm." This name is wholly undeserved; for Korea is seldom at peace, being always disturbed by warfare either at home or with some neighbor. It is a rich country, because the soil is fertile and produces heavy crops of rice, millet, etc. Besides this, the rivers contain much gold and the mountains are full of minerals. But the people are wretchedly poor, because the officers rob them of all they have.

For a very long time this people refused to have anything to do with us. They fired on our ships when near their coast, and it was not until 1882 that they consented to make a treaty with us. Since that time Americans have been allowed to live in Korea. Now, you might think from this that the Koreans are a brave people, but they are not. They do not like to fight, and besides they are very lazy. It is not often that you see them at work. They smoke long pipes, and lounge all day in the streets or on the roads, dressed in long white cotton garments, and stiff hats made of horse-hair. They manage to get just enough to live on, and that is all they care for, because they know that if they save anything, their officers will come and take it from them. But it was not always thus. At the time that Empress Jingu thought of invading their country, the Koreans were great workers in wood and metals, and made many fine objects. They first taught the Japanese, but that people improved, while the Koreans have forgotten all they ever knew.

After Empress Jingu had determined upon war with Korea, she did not lose any time in making her preparations. War junks were built, and a great army was raised. The soldiers were told to meet at the west coast of the island of Kiushiu, where they were to go on board. The empress herself was to take the command, and she had no doubt that she would be able to seize Korea.

She stood, you must know, in great favor with the Dragon King, who lived in the World Under the Sea, and she was confident that this powerful sea god would help her. To be sure, there might be some of the sea gods who would be favorable to the Koreans, but then the Dragon King was the most powerful, and he would know how to discover and set at naught any tricks these lesser gods might be inclined to play.

And she was not mistaken. Before she embarked, the Dragon King presented her with two crystal balls, having exactly the same power as the jewels which Prince Put-the-Fire-Out had received from his father-in-law. If she threw one of them into the sea, the water would rise to a great height, and if she cast the other one in, the water would flow out again until the bed of the sea appeared. You may think that these would be rather dangerous toys to play with; but Empress Jingu knew how to handle them, as you will hear.

The fleet set sail, and had hardly lost sight of the land when a tempest arose, and the waves became threatening. This was, of course, caused by some sea god who favored the Koreans. But if Jingu's friend, the Dragon King, could not prevent such a mishap, he could at least see to it that no harm was done. So he quietly ordered some large fish, such as sharks, porpoises, etc., to harness themselves to Jingu's vessels, and tow them to Korea. It was no wonder, therefore, that, storm or no storm, the Japanese fleet arrived safe near the coast of Korea.

The king of Korea had heard all about Jingu and her preparations, and was ready to meet her. He had drawn up his army on the beach, and was watching to see whether the Japanese would try to effect a landing. But Jingu knew what she was about. After her ships had been securely anchored, she gave the necessary orders, and warned her warriors not to be surprised at anything that might happen. When everything was ready, she dropped one of the crystal balls into the sea, and the water began to run out, until the ships stuck fast in the mud.

When the king of Korea saw this, he thought that he had the Japanese at his mercy. He gave orders to his army to charge, and they made straight for the enemy's vessels. When they were at some distance from the shore, Jingu dropped the other ball, and the water began to rush back. The Koreans had no time to reach either the dry land or the vessels, and their king saw his army drowned before his eyes, and his country at the mercy of his enemy. What could he do but submit? Empress Jingu led her army in triumph to his capital, and the king was compelled to make peace on her terms. They were that the king must hand over to Japan eighty vessels loaded with gold, silver, and other valuables, and give hostages that he would pay her a tribute every year.

Some people think that there is about as much truth in the story of Empress Jingu and her invasion of Korea, as in that of the sun goddess and her son. But there is one fact that is worth knowing, and that is that there is an extraordinary ebb and flood upon the Korean coast; in some places the water rises to a height of thirty-two feet, while at low tide, the ocean bed is dry for more than a mile from the shore.

The Japanese claimed for a long time that this conquest gave them a right upon the peninsula. And you will read later how this claim led to many a serious rebellion, and finally to the war with China.

BUDDHISM BROUGHT TO JAPAN

THE Japanese must believe that their emperor is a god. They are allowed to believe anything else besides this, and neither the emperor nor the government cares, so long as they remain faithful in that one point. When, therefore, missionaries from other countries come, they are allowed to preach whatever they please, but if any one should dare express a doubt about the emperor's being a god, the punishment would be swift and sure.

In the seventh century such missionaries came from Korea, and taught the Japanese how to work in metal and in wood, to make porcelain, and to raise silkworms and make silk. The Japanese were very glad to learn all this, for they are an industrious people, and always glad to be taught anything that may benefit them. But some of these missionaries also preached a new religion, and told them that Buddha (boo-dah) was the greatest of all gods. Some of the Japanese liked this new religion, and became Buddhists, that is, believers in Buddha. This did not at all interfere with their belief in the emperor. The missionaries had brought with them images of Buddha, and they wanted temples in which to place them. So one nobleman gave them his house and they made a temple of it. But it happened that just then a pestilence swept over the country, and it was rumored that the emperor's ancestors, who had all become gods, were angry at having a rival. So the people burned this new temple and flung the image of Buddha into the sea. But after that another pestilence broke out; and besides this, there was a severe earthquake, and a flood which drowned a great many people along the coast. This frightened the people, for they imagined that Buddha was angry. So they built a new temple, and afterwards a great many more.

Until the missionaries came, the Japanese did not know how to read and write. The Koreans had learned these arts from the Chinese, and they now taught them to the people of Japan. Chinese writing is very difficult to learn; for instead of having letters from which all words can be formed, the Chinese have a character for each separate word. But the Japanese are hard students and learn quickly, so they not only mastered the Chinese way of writing, but later went one step farther; they modified the signs and made them stand for sounds, and now they have, in addition to their characters representing words, a syllabary or table of forty-seven signs for syllables. Books were brought over from Korea, and very soon the Japanese began to write the history of their country, a part of which I have told you.

All this made great changes in Japan. Up to this time, every able-bodied man had been a warrior whenever war broke out. But now only the strongest were taken, and the old and weak were left to till the rice fields or to engage in other business. The warriors were the most powerful of all the people. Next in rank came the farmers, then the mechanics, and last of all, the merchants or traders.

But the greatest change was in the court of the emperor. There had been no war for some time, and the emperors having little to do, passed their time in reading the books brought over from Korea. That they might not be disturbed, they appointed ministers to attend to the collection of the taxes, to see that the people kept at their work, to protect the weak, and to punish offenders. So, after some time, these ministers grew accustomed to have all the power, and when a new emperor ascended the throne who showed signs that he wanted to reign himself, his ministers quickly had his head shaved; that is, they made a Buddhist priest of him, shut him up in a convent or cloister, and put his son, if he had any, or else some nephew or cousin, on the throne.

The people did not know anything of what was going on in the big palace where the emperor lived. They were taught and believed firmly that he was a god, and his ministers took good care that he was never seen outside the walls around the palace grounds. If he ever did go out, he was placed in a sort of cage fastened to a bullock cart, and hidden from view by bamboo curtains. The houses of each street through which he passed were ordered to be closed, and the windows covered with shutters; and those who happened to be in such a street were compelled to kneel down, their hands fiat on the ground before them, and their heads bent low upon the hands. Most of the emperors from that time on were mere babies, who, as soon as they were old enough to show a will of their own, were quickly and quietly placed in a convent. But you will see, as we proceed, that the men who were in power did not use their authority to oppress the people and make themselves rich. They thought what they did was best for Japan, and they did not care for wealth.

The first real capital was at Nara (nah-rah). If ever you visit Japan, you must not fail to make an excursion to this place, which is within a short distance of Kyoto (kee-yoh-toh) and Osaka (oh-sah-kah). It is situated in the south-central part of the island of Hondo, in a most beautiful spot, on the edge of a fertile plain surrounded by mountains. You may still see the long avenues of old trees, and some of the grand temples, once so plentiful, but now so few that the Japanese call them "ruins among the rice fields." Those that are left have finely colored paintings and images of gilded bronze; and near one of them is a huge statue of Buddha, also made of bronze. At eventide you will hear a loud and melodious booming. It is from the great bell, struck at that time, and on calm days it can be heard at a distance of twenty miles.

From Nara the capital was transferred to Kyoto, also in a most beautiful location. All foreigners coming to Japan are certain to visit that old city, which remained the capital until 1868. There they find not only a great number of temples, but streets with stores, where the finest products of Japanese art are for sale. There are dainty silks, beautifully carved metals, porcelain,—so thin that it is almost transparent,—and articles in lacquer ware, for which these people are famous all over the world. And with all this, it is such a queer city! There are houses nestling on crags against the mountain side. And if you go at night near the dry bed of the river, you may witness a scene that seems as if taken from the Arabian Nights,—thousands of booths, each lit up with the many-colored paper lanterns, a countless number of which seem to be flitting to and fro. These lanterns are carried by people who go in and out of the booths, where they seem to be having a perpetual picnic. For the Japanese, when they go out after dark, always carry a lighted lantern, to prevent accidents.

But now, as the court is established in quaint old Kyoto, I must tell you of the clans of Japan.

THE OLDEST CLANS OF JAPAN

IF an emperor had more than one son, the younger sons would, if they married and had children, become the founders of noble houses. Thus, in the course of time, a nobility was formed, the members of which were, or claimed to be, descendants of a former Tennô. And just as the nobles of Europe had a family coat of arms, so did the nobles of Japan adopt some flower or animal by which the members of their family or clan could be known.

The three principal clans at this time were the Fujiwara (foo-jee-wah-rah), whose emblem was the blue wistaria, the Minamoto (mee-nah-moh-toh) with the white gentian as emblem, and the Taira (ti-rah), whose coat of arms was a red butterfly. The head of each clan was usually called by the clan name. At first the Fujiwara clan held the power behind the throne and the head of this house was the man who for a long time selected the emperor or made him retire to a cloister, according to his docility in obeying the orders of the Fujiwara. All the offices among the people were occupied by members of this clan; that is, all the civil offices, for the army was in command of two other clans. The Minamoto clan were intrusted with the subduing of the independent tribes in the northern part of Hondo, and, after many years of fighting, succeeded. The Taira were engaged in destroying the pirates who infested the Inland Sea; that is, the sea between Hondo, Shikoku (shee-kohk), and Kiushiu.

But after the pirates had disappeared and the whole of the island of Hondo had been brought under the rule of the Tennô, the Minamoto and Taira returned to the capital, and when they saw the influence and power of the Fujiwara, they became very jealous. Yet, so great was the respect for the dignity of the Tennô, that neither of the two great military clans, powerful and strong as they were, ventured to oppose the ruling clan. But in the twelfth century something happened that gave the Taira an opportunity to interfere, and swords flew out of their scabbards, and blood flowed, while the country was first made acquainted with the horrors of a civil war.

The emperor was dead. He had been a puppet in the hands of the Fujiwara, but on his deathbed he left the throne to his elder brother, instead of to his baby son. This did not suit the ruling clan at all, and they called upon the Minamoto to aid them in placing the baby emperor upon the throne. But the brother of the late emperor insisted upon his rights, and asked the Taira to help him. The head of this clan, a very able and ambitious man, was but too anxious to secure the influence held by the Fujiwara by placing an emperor upon the throne. So a great battle was fought in Kyoto in which the Fujiwara and the Minamoto were defeated, and the Taira secured the throne for the rightful heir.

But as soon as they had succeeded in doing this, they locked the emperor up as tightly as the Fujiwara had done before; and when the Tennô, who seems to have been really an able man, protested against this treatment, Taira had his head shaved, and sent him off to a cloister, after which he placed an eighteen-year-old boy upon the throne.

Now, some of the members of the Minamoto clan had helped the Taira, because they were jealous of the power of the Fujiwara. But when Taira was in power, he acted with such cruelty against the Minamoto that the members of the two defeated clans entered into a conspiracy against him. Taira, however, was wide awake. Long before all the plans of the conspirators were completed, the members of the Minamoto were attacked in the streets of Kyoto. No mercy was asked or given, and again blood flowed freely. Indeed, so well did Taira do his work, that he destroyed almost the entire clan of the Minamoto. The head of that unfortunate clan escaped for a short time, but was discovered by one of the Taira, and murdered.

The new regent—for such he was in reality, because the emperor was not consulted in any act pertaining to the government—now discharged nearly all the officers of the Fujiwara, and filled their places with members of his own clan. The people were not consulted, and did not care much. For even at that time, while every clan liked to be in power, its members never sought office for gain but did their work honestly and well.

MINAMOTO DEFEATS TAIRA

TAIRA was established in Kyoto, and thought himself pretty safe,—not wholly so, though, for two young sons of Minamoto had escaped, and so had one of his wives. He suspected, naturally, that the two children would be with her, and to get them in his power he had the widow's mother arrested, and made it known far and near that she would be put to death unless her daughter came back and surrendered herself. Now you must know that in Japan the highest and first duty of children is toward their parents. There are a great many instances of children who have sold themselves into slavery to save their parents from want. Indeed, the same thing happens often enough in these days, and the law allows it. The Japanese applaud these examples of filial piety. We, too, are taught the commandment, "Honor thy father and thy mother"; but we consider that other duties are as important, as, for instance, the duty of a father or a mother toward a child, or of a husband toward his wife. These are as nothing in Japan compared to the child's duty toward a parent.

When the poor young widow heard of the arrest of her mother, she did not hesitate. One of the boys, Yoritomo, the head of the Minamoto, had been separated from her in the flight, and for all she knew he might have been captured or killed. In that event her son, Yoshitsune (yoh-shee-tsoo-nay) would become heir to the Minamoto, and with him that famous family would die out. She could not expect mercy from a man who had shown so much cruelty; still she did not hesitate, but retraced her steps, and surrendered herself and her son to the Taira.

In the meanwhile Yoritomo had wandered among the fugitives and pursuers. He was brought before a captain of the victors, and the latter soon discovered who his young prisoner was. The capture was important, and the captain returned to Kyoto with his prisoner. Taira was about to give orders to put him to death, when his mother interfered, and asked him to spare the child's life. Her request was granted, and Yoritomo was given to his captor, who took him to his home in the southern part of Japan.

When Minamoto's widow was led before the victor, he was struck both with her beauty and her filial conduct, and when, with tears in her eyes, she begged for the life of her child, he did not find it in his heart to refuse her. So he ordered the little boy to be taken to a convent, where, when he was old enough, his head was to be shaved and he was to be made a priest.

Yoritomo grew up in the family of his captor, and became skillful in the exercises of the privileged class. He thought frequently of the misfortunes of his clan, and was forever planning schemes of revenge. His foster father had two daughters, and the more beautiful of the two he had promised to the son of a friend. Yoritomo and this girl fell in love with each other, and they decided to elope. As the girl was her father's favorite, she had no doubt that she would be forgiven. She was not mistaken; for not only were the young couple kindly received when they returned, but the bride induced her father, Hojo (hoh-joh), to assist Yoritomo in his schemes.

What had become in the meanwhile of Yoritomo's half-brother, Yoshitsune, who had been placed in the convent? As he grew up, the priests gave him the nickname of "Young Ox," on account of his great strength. They had a hard time with him, for he did not mind them in the least. Although they could not keep him in check, and he was continually playing tricks upon them, they did not dare bring a complaint before the regent. But when, at last, he made his escape in the company of a peddler, they were so glad to be rid of him that they did not try very hard to get him back.

Young Ox made his way to the northern part of the island of Hondo, where he was taken into the service of the governor, one of the few Fujiwara men who had been kept in office. He grew up to be as brave as he was strong, and he, too, remembered, the unhappy fate of his clan, and tried to communicate with all those who had been fortunate enough to escape the slaughter.

Yoritomo himself was impatient to avenge his wrongs. After he had collected a small band, he made for the Hakone Mountains, not far from the place where Prince Bravest had lost his wife. But his plans had become known, and he was attacked and defeated by a strong force of the Taira. He sought safety in flight, hotly pursued by his enemies. When night fell, he found shelter in a hollow tree. He had been there but a short time, when a band of the pursuers approached, and scattered to search the wood. One of them came near his tree, but seeing a wood pigeon fly from her nest, concluded that no one could be there because the bird had not been disturbed.

When morning came, no enemy was to be seen, and Yoritomo continued his flight. After walking all day, he saw, just as it was getting dark, a little house. On entering, he found it tenanted by a priest, who scanned him closely, and gave him to understand that he suspected who he was. Upon this, Yoritomo took the priest into his confidence, and it was well that he did so, for his host insisted upon his hiding in an obscure closet. During the night they were awakened by threatening voices, and when the priest opened the door, several Taira warriors inquired whether any strangers were in the house. The priest invited them to search for themselves, but after taking a cursory glance over the poor apartments, they continued their march.

The next morning, after thanking his preserver, Yoritomo made his way to, a small peninsula, where he continued his plotting, and soon succeeded in collecting another band. Again he made for the Hakone Mountains, and once more he was defeated. But now the fame; of his exploits had spread over the land, and when he withdrew again to the peninsula, large numbers of his own clan, who had kept in hiding, flocked to his standard, as well as many of the Fujiwara.

Among the first to come was Young Ox, who led a strong force of able-bodied warriors whom he had collected in the north. The brothers were glad to see each other, although they did not show their feelings openly, since it is against the custom of the country to evince emotion. A cousin also brought a number of men, and Yoritomo now thought that he was strong enough to take the field. He divided his army into three parts. The van was placed in command of his cousin; and was stationed in the mountains between Kamakura (kah-mah'-koo-rah) and Kyoto; the center under Young Ox held "Kamakura, while Yoritomo himself commanded the rear, and continued to enlist fresh arrivals.

Before proceeding, I must tell you something about Kamakura. It is only a short distance from Yokohama and can be reached by railroad. It is a lovely valley inclosed by mountains, but opening upon the sea. It contains several large Buddhist temples, and an immense bronze statue of Buddha which the Japanese call Dai Butsu (di-boots), or Great Buddha.

All this time Taira was gathering his clan to crush his opponent. He reproached himself bitterly for having spared the two boys, and finally fell sick. He grew worse and worse, and when he was convinced that he was dying, he called his son and said, "Do not waste any time on funeral ceremonies, or offer any sacrifices to me; but cut off the head of Yoritomo and put it on my tomb."

As soon as Yoritomo's cousin heard of the death of the regent, he set out for the capital, without waiting for instructions. The Taira troops were superior in number, but they had not yet recovered from the confusion incident upon the death of their leader; and when they were attacked under the walls of the city by the van of Yoritomo's army, the regent's troops wavered. Perceiving this, the assailants redoubled their efforts. It was as if every single warrior fancied himself the avenger of the wrongs suffered by his clan for so many years, and at last the regent's forces were routed. The capital was taken, and Taira fled, taking with him the young emperor and his mother. Yoritomo's cousin, however, found a seven-year-old brother of the emperor in the palace. He proclaimed this child emperor and appointed himself as regent, intending to secure the chieftainship of the Minamoto clan.

THE STORY OF 'YOUNG OX'

WHEN the young lord of the clan heard of the events that had taken place in the capital, he left the peninsula and marched upon Kamakura. Here he found Young Ox with the center of his army, and ordered him to go at once to Kyoto to punish their treacherous cousin. The latter was informed by spies of the approach of this army, and he led his victorious troops to a little village south of Kyoto on the Yodo (yoh-doh) River, and there awaited the attack. He had not long to wait. His troops, recognizing the wrong of their leader's cause, fought in a half-hearted way, and he was defeated. While he was trying to effect his escape, his horse floundered in the mud of a rice field, and he was shot in the forehead with an arrow.

Young Ox now turned his attention to the Taira, who had escaped from the capital. The young lord of that clan had taken refuge in a castle near Kobe (koh-bay), but Young Ox took it by assault, and it was with difficulty that Taira escaped and hurried to another castle of his clan, which was also taken. The fugitive, accompanied by the empress and the boy emperor, now decided upon seeking a shelter in the island of Kiushiu. With the remnant of his clan he embarked in as many ships as he could collect, and set sail.

But Young Ox was not to be balked of his prey. He incited his followers to the greatest efforts, and in a short time succeeded in assembling enough vessels to embark his army and set off in pursuit. In the straits at the west entrance to the Inland Sea, the fugitives were overtaken. A naval battle was fought in which the troops of Taira fought with the courage of despair, but to no avail. Young Ox remained victor. A few of the clan who effected their escape sought refuge in the mountain fastnesses of the island of Kiushiu. The empress, unwilling to surrender, jumped into the sea with the, boy emperor, and both were drowned.

After defeating the enemies of his half-brother, Young Ox returned to Kamakura. You would naturally suppose that the young lord would welcome the hero who had rendered him and his clan such important services; but not so. It may be that Yoritomo was afraid that his half-brother might have ambitious plans, such as his cousin had; or perhaps he was jealous of the glory and fame gained by Young Ox. At any rate, when the victorious army approached Kamakura, the head of the clan sent a messenger to Young Ox with the order to encamp beyond the city walls, and there to deliver up the trophies and spoils. Young Ox obeyed without a murmur, and, receiving an order to that effect, withdrew with his army to Kyoto.

He was but a short time in the capital when his command was taken from him, and he noticed that he could not leave the house without being followed by spies. He began to fear that he would be poisoned or stabbed if he remained in Kyoto, so he moved to a small country place, taking care not to arouse suspicion. He lived by himself and saw no one, but he was still watched by spies. At last he decided to return to the north of Japan to the place where he had first plotted against Taira, which he had left only to help his brother. Here he would not be suspected, and he was satisfied to withdraw from public life, since he had avenged the wrongs of his clan. So Young Ox left for the north without meeting with any adventures, and arrived at his old refuge. But the old governor was dead, and his place was held by his son, who, to court favor with the new regent, had the young hero assassinated.

If the cowardly murderer had expected a reward, he was much disappointed, for he was tried and executed by order of Minamoto. But this did not prevent tongues from wagging; and it was rumored that the new regent was not entirely innocent of his brother's murder.

Yoritomo was now regent. He had entered Kyoto in triumph, and had received the title and rank from the baby emperor whom his cousin had placed on the throne. The regent, however, declined to reside in the capital. He left a trusty officer to watch over the emperor; that is, to prevent any other clan from obtaining control over his person. After he had secured a deed by which the title and power of regent should remain in his family, Yoritomo set about restoring order, the country having been much disturbed by the civil war.

Buddhist cloisters and convents had greatly multiplied, and the monks did not like to see the emperor a mere puppet in the hands of a great clan. So they made as much difficulty for the regent as they could. But after Yoritomo had burned a few of their cloisters, the monks saw that he was too strong for them, and they submitted to his laws.

After Yoritomo had punished robbers, and made the roads safe for travelers and merchants, he began to encourage the arts and industries. It was during his reign that the Dai Butsu, the great bronze statue of Buddha, was cast. The Japanese became wonderfully skillful in metal working. They were especially famous for the temper of the swords they made.

THE LAST OF THE MINAMOTO

YORITOMO died suddenly from the effect of a fall from his horse, and was succeeded by his son, who, however, was not yet of age. His mother's father, Hojo, was appointed as his guardian. You remember that this old man had been a captain in the Taira clan, but that his daughter had persuaded him to help Yoritomo. Hojo had remained faithful to his son-in-law, of whom he was somewhat afraid. But now that the regent was dead, the captain made up his mind to be the real regent, even if his grandson held the title.

But when the son of Yoritomo grew up to man's estate, he wanted to rule as his father had done before him, and would not be satisfied with the mere honors and rank of regent. So his grandfather quietly ordered his head to be shaved, and sent him off to a cloister, where he was locked up. And when even within the walls of this prison,—for such it was,—he continued to protest against the actions of his grandfather, he was murdered by order of the captain, and his younger brother was made regent.

Now, until within recent years, Japanese boys were wont to marry very young, and so you will not wonder that the poor murdered regent had left a son, who brooded over the violent death of his father. When this lad was old enough to handle a sword, he attacked his uncle, the new regent, and killed him. Hereupon Hojo condemned him to death, and the boy was executed.

Yoritomo had no other sons, and you might think that the family had died out. But you would be mistaken. In Japan it is the custom when there are no male heirs in a family, to adopt a child, who takes the name of his foster father and has all the rights and privileges of a son. Hence there was no difficulty to provide a new regent: all that had to be done was to adopt a baby, and the widow of Yoritomo wrote to Kyoto to have one sent.

"But," you will ask, "why did not this widow interfere with her father to prevent the murder of her oldest son, and the execution of her grandson?" If you have not forgotten what I have said of the filial duties of a Japanese, you will know that the mother was in duty bound to yield blind obedience to her father. His will was law, and it would have violated every Japanese principle if she had dared oppose him in any of his resolutions.

Another question you are apt to ask is what the faithful Minamoto clansmen did when they saw the family of their lord ruthlessly slaughtered by one who belonged to their foes, the Taira. To this I must answer that the old captain was sly enough to keep the death of a regent secret until he had another one safe and sound on the throne. And the clansmen were satisfied as long as they knew that a head of the Minamoto was, in name at least, the regent. They obeyed, not him, but the orders issued over his name and seal.

The loyalty of a Japanese is intense; it is so strong that he will shrink from no danger, and will even commit suicide when the order is given by those who have lawful authority. But until the revolution of 1868 this loyalty was to the clan as a political body, and not to the head of the clan personally. It was the crest or seal that was revered as the personification of the clan, and if the official documents containing commands bore the seal of the clan, they were obeyed without hesitation, whoever might be the temporary head that issued them.

From what I have said here, you will understand why the Taira captain, who was without doubt the actual ruler of Japan, did not dare proclaim himself as regent, and why he and his descendants continued to place on the regent's throne at Kamakura babies, who are known in Japanese history as "shadow regents," because they were regents only in name. And this will further explain how the Japanese writers of history of this day boast, in good faith, of the loyalty of the people for the emperor and his family, while at the same time they tell the story much as I have told it to you thus far. And the people were loyal, according to their idea; that is, they obeyed cheerfully any order given under the crest and seal of the Tennô. And when they did take up arms against him, it was with no disloyalty, for they announced that they were fighting only against his advisers; that is, against the men who used his crest and seal to further their own schemes. The story of Japan is not easy to understand; but if you can remember what I have said above, you will find less difficulty.

You will see now that, even at this early time, the Tennô had no real power; that the country was ruled by regents from Kamakura as the capital; and that the man who could make and depose the regents was the real ruler of people, regent, and emperor.

AN INDEPENDENT TENNÔ

AS you have read before, Yoritomo's father-in-law was named Hojo, which means either a Buddhist priest or a convent, or one who sets free a live animal that has been caught. For you must know that the Buddhists believe that the souls of men go after death into the bodies of animals. That is why faithful believers in Buddha will not eat the flesh of animals. They say, "How does one know that the soul of his father or grandfather may not have been in the body of the ox that is killed?"

The Hojo family ruled over Japan one hundred and fourteen years, always in the name of some shadow regent. But although they had no right to rule the country, the Hojo were good and just to the people, and helped the progress of arts and industries, so that Japan grew to be a rich country.

It was during the Hojo period (1199-1333) that the famous Japanese swords were first made. Before this the two-edged blade had been used, which was but a clumsy weapon to strike with; but the swords made during the Hojo period would cut through a dollar without leaving a flaw. In 1877 there was a dangerous, rebellion in Japan. The government troops were armed with modern rifles and balls, and many of the rebels had only their swords. But they killed so many of the regular troops with these dangerous weapons that the government was compelled to form a troop of expert swordsmen to cope with them.

The Hojo also kept up the army. The soldiers of Japan had now become a distinct caste, that is, only certain families could serve in war, and their sons were also soldiers. They were called samurai (sah-moo-ri), and had the right to wear two swords. The long two-handled one was used in war. The other, short as a dagger, was for nothing else than to commit suicide. At first it was used only after a battle, when a wounded soldier, preferring death to falling into the hands of the enemy, stabbed himself with the short sword. But soon it became a privilege of the samurai class to commit suicide when they had done anything for which the common people would have been condemned to death. The sons of samurai were taught in early youth how to behave themselves and what to do if ever the time should come when they would have to commit hara-kiri (hah-rah'-kee-ree—hara is the Japanese word for stomach, and kiri means to cut). By this kind of education, they grew familiar with the idea of dying at any time. Soon it became such a custom, that when a clan was insulted, and for some reason could not take revenge, the principal samurai would commit hara-kiri in a dignified manner, and so wipe out the stain upon the crest of the clan.

The Hojo were proud of their country, and loved it, as every Japanese does. They ruled, honestly thinking that it was best for Japan that they should do so. When the Chinese emperor sent two men to demand that Japan should pay tribute, thereby confessing that the emperor of China was really their master, the reigning Hojo ordered the messengers' heads to be cut off, as an answer to the insolent demand. The Chinese emperor was so angry at this that he gathered a great army and fleet to take Japan, but he was badly defeated. So the Hojo do not deserve the dislike with which they are regarded by the people, who call a bug that destroys the young rice by the name of Hojo bug.

But now I must tell you how the Hojo rule came to an end through the efforts of an emperor who would not be a mere puppet. The poor babies or boys who had held the title of Tennô had been much neglected, and when one of them died, the court had not sufficient money for funeral ceremonies, so that he had to be buried by charity. At last the Hojo, in their turn, became puppets, and Japan was ruled by some ex-regent, who had retired to a cloister; and for some time the monks were the ruling power. But although they held an unlawful authority, they were inclined to restore the government to the emperor.

In the early part of the fourteenth century, the Tennô died, and the Hojo placed upon the throne a prince, named Godaigo (goh-di-goh), from whom they expected no trouble. He seemed to care for nothing except pleasure, and that was the sort of man they wanted. But this prince had only pretended to be of such disposition, for he was really a man of courage and ability. When the government at Kamakura discovered this, they decided that he must abdicate, and they sent an army to the capital. The emperor not having enough troops to defend Kyoto, withdrew with his band to a Buddhist cloister not far from Nara, which had been strongly fortified. But the regent was determined to maintain his power. His army set out in pursuit, carried the cloister by assault, and captured the emperor. He was sent into exile, and the heads of his advisers were cut off, and carried on poles fastened to his sedan chair.

But this emperor was a man of strong will, and, while in exile, he sent letters to one of his sons, who was a Buddhist priest, and to one of his captains, who had escaped with a small body of faithful troops. After everything was prepared, the emperor left the island to which he had been banished, escaping in a fishing boat, and hiding himself under a heap of mussels. He was missed, and the boat was pursued and overtaken; but the mussel heap was not searched, and the emperor reached the island of Hondo, where he was joined by a small army. With this he marched at once upon Kyoto, and as the Hojo commander was unprepared, the capital was captured.

The Hojo now sent more troops against him, but their leaders, who were members of the old Minamoto clan, went over to the emperor, and many who had been kept away, through fear of the power of the Hojo, now joined the imperial standard. One of the Minamoto leaders, in command of the emperor's army, advanced upon Kamakura. The Hojo made a desperate defense. The outer walls were carried by assault, but every ward had been made into a fortress, and the place was taken only after a furious hand-to-hand fight. When the Hojo clan were utterly defeated, their leaders took their own lives by the dreadful hara-kiri, and once more it seemed as though the Tennô would regain his power.

But it was not to be. The two Minamoto leaders who had betrayed the Hojo regent, began to quarrel, and one of them denounced his former comrade to the emperor, accusing the man who had taken Kamakura of designs against the Tennô. But this general succeeded in proving his innocence, whereupon the emperor commissioned him to punish his traducer. A battle was fought between the two former comrades in arms, in which the emperor's troops were defeated, and the poor Heaven Child was again compelled to flee from the capital. Once more he took refuge in the convent where he had been captured by the Hojo troops.

And now the victorious leader, whose family name was Ashikaga (ash-ee-kah-gah), took the title and office of regent. He did not pursue the emperor, for the generals who had remained loyal gave him enough to do. First the regent pursued his former friend, and attacked him with a very strong force northwest of Kyoto, and he not only defeated his troops, but killed their leader. Then Ashikaga attacked the capital, which was taken and retaken three times. Then the last faithful band retired upon Hiogo, where they were finally routed and their leader committed the inevitable hara-kiri. The regent now appointed a puppet emperor in Kyoto, and left the other Tennô to rule, if he chose, over the monks in the convent. For time there were two Tennôs in Japan. But after a while the real emperor resigned in favor of the puppet emperor at Kyoto, who had after all no more power than his rival.

CHRISTIANITY IN JAPAN

THE history of Japan, from this time, becomes very interesting. It is known among the Japanese as the period of the Ashikaga regents (1338-1574). These rulers were worse than any the country had ever had. They did not have the firm hand of the Hojo. Military governors were appointed over the provinces, and most of them, seeing that they had nothing to fear from the incapable regents, declared themselves independent. So these governors became chiefs, their sons succeeded them, and the former province became their territory. They made war upon each other, and sometimes, when one of them was powerful enough, he would set up an opposition regent.

By these unhappy conditions the people suffered most. Their rice fields were trampled down by invading or retreating bands, their harvests, if they had any, were destroyed, and their homes were ruined. Kyoto and other cities were taken and plundered by bands of free lances, robbers were masters on the highways, and pirates made the seas and rivers unsafe.

But the Buddhist convents grew rich and powerful as they had never been before, for a great many of the monks knew how to handle sword and bow and arrow, and turned soldier whenever the occasion offered. One of them, who is known as "the Fighting Abbot," took two provinces; and the strong castle of Osaka—one of the points of interest in Japan at the present day—was built by these priests. The stones of most of this fortress are of such immense size that one wonders how the priests succeeded in raising them one upon the other, without any machinery. It is quite sure that these Buddhist monks would at last have become the rulers of Japan, had they not taken to fighting among themselves. These quarrelsome habits did not at all increase love for them among the people, while the chieftains, as the successors of the military governors must now be called, were jealous of the wealth, power, and influence of the priesthood.

This time—for we have now reached in our history the sixteenth century period—was the age of great discoveries. Marco Polo, in the thirteenth century, had visited China, which he called Cathay, and had heard there of the island empire to the northeast, of which he wrote under the name of Zipangu (zee-pon-goo). In 1497, Vasco da Gama had sailed round the southern point of Africa, the Cape of Good Hope, and had reached India. It was with the idea of finding a short route to Cathay, or China, that Columbus had sailed westward, and he would have succeeded had not the American continent been in his way.

The Portuguese sailors of those days were very enterprising, and no sooner had they discovered one country, than they set out to find another. They were brave seamen, for the ships were very small. Their main object was to get rich by trading with the newly discovered countries, but they also wished to convert the heathen people to Christianity.

After the Portuguese had come to China, they went to seek Japan. Now you must remember that the Japanese in the sixteenth century were a very civilized people; they had a regular government, tilled the ground or lived in cities and villages, and knew a great deal of the arts and industries. Besides this, their soldiers were brave and loved their country, even if they did fight among themselves.

But, as I have said, the power acquired by the Buddhist convents had caused a deep feeling of hatred against them, both among the daimio (di-mee-yoh), as the chieftains were called, and the people; and the first Portuguese priest who came to Japan was a very good man, who is known in history as St. Francis Xavier (zav'-i-er).

His first landing was made in Kiushiu in 1542, and he was well received by the diamio. To his astonishment, he found the Japanese in possession of matchlocks, as the guns of those days were called. He learned afterwards that a Portuguese named Mendez Pinto (men-deth peen-toh), who had visited Japan a short time previously, had made them a present of such a gun, and the Japanese, who are remarkable for their power of imitation, had set to work and made a number of these arms.

St. Francis Xavier found attentive hearers in the Japanese among whom he preached; and as the daimio did nothing to oppose his efforts, Christianity very soon began to spread among them. After some time this missionary crossed over to Hondo, and visited the capital of the Tennô. He had expected to find a rich and flourishing city, but the troubled times had left an imprint upon Kyoto, and he saw nothing more than an armed camp.

Several of the daimio, who had become converted, sent representatives to the pope. They crossed the Pacific Ocean in a Japanese vessel, and landed in Mexico; after traveling through that country, they sailed for Spain, and from there reached Italy. There are now in the museum in Madrid two fine specimens of the suits of armor worn by Japanese samurai in those days. They were given to King Philip II by this embassy. A few years ago the Japanese ambassador found in Venice a stone bearing an inscription which showed that this same Japanese embassy had visited that city.

Several Portuguese missionaries came after St. Francis Xavier, and they succeeded, after many years, in making quite a number of converts. But other nations of Europe were anxious to trade with Japan, and among these were the Hollanders, who had risen in rebellion against Spain. I cannot tell you here about the causes that led to this or of the events that followed. But I must mention that the Spaniards conquered Portugal, so that from that time all the Portuguese possessions belonged to Spain, and their ships sailed under the Spanish flag. The Hollanders now made war upon Portuguese ships and colonies, and began to lay schemes to have the Portuguese expelled from Japan. We shall hereafter see how they succeeded.

The Ashikaga rule had been very bad for Japan, and one of these weak regents submitted to a demand from the emperor of China, and paid tribute. Japanese boys and men feel very badly when they read this part of their history. Their books say that this money was given to pay for damages done by Japanese pirates, who skimmed over the western coast of the Pacific Ocean, and attacked not only cities in China, but went as far south as Siam. The fact is that the money was paid, and that these regents were justly blamed for the disgrace brought upon their country. But now I must tell you how these rulers were driven out, and a new line took charge of the government.

A GREAT GENERAL

A POOR priest in one of the villages of Japan had a son named Nobunaga (noh-boo-nah'-gah). This priest claimed that his ancestor was the great Taira who had ruled over Japan; he said that when the Taira were hunted down by the Minamoto, the widow of one of Taira's sons fled with her little boy to a small village, whose mayor afterwards married her. After some time it happened that a priest, passing through the village, saw the boy and took a fancy to him. He went to see the mother and father, and obtained their consent to take the boy with him. He promised that he would give him a good education and make a priest of him. This man kept his word. The boy grew up to be a priest and married, and became the ancestor of Nobunaga and his father.

The boy, Nobunaga, was a great fighter, and was shrewd besides. He did not like the way the country was governed, and although his father himself was a priest, the son disliked the convents and looked with disfavor on the power and wealth which they had acquired. He enlisted as a warrior when but a boy, and was so brave and skillful in war that he was still young when he had taken a province and made himself a daimio, or lord. But he was not yet satisfied. He continued making war upon his neighbors until he had captured three other provinces, one of which was near the old capital Kyoto. And now something happened that gave him the opportunity to enter the capital with his army.

The Ashikaga regent was murdered in the year 1574. This, in itself, was not very remarkable, for it happened often enough in those days, and really the country did not suffer any loss; but it was a murder, and our friend Nobunaga said that murder was a crime, and must be punished. He declared also that the late regent's brother had the right to succeed him, and that he, Nobunaga, would see justice done. He was as good as his word. He entered the capital and appointed the regent: but he made himself vice regent, which means that he did the governing and that the other was only a puppet.

But Nobunaga had work to do, and it was work that required great energy and a firm hand. First of all, the fighting among the great daimio or chieftains had to be stopped. This was not so very difficult, for since they quarreled among themselves, they were not powerful enough to oppose the vice regent's well-drilled troops. But he had more difficulty in dealing with the powerful Buddhist convents. The city of Osaka, about thirty-seven miles from the capital, Kyoto, had been fortified by them. Five powerful castles, having strong connections, defended this city. After a long siege, he captured three of these castles, but the other two held out, and he tried to starve them into surrender. When at last the inmates were suffering from famine, they attempted to cut their way through the besiegers during the night, but they were driven back after showing the greatest courage.

Now Nobunaga was threatened in his rear. He had left only a small garrison at Kyoto, and was informed that one of the daimio and an army of monks from the wealthiest convent of Japan had marched upon the capital. Leaving a sufficient number of troops before Osaka, he himself hastened to the relief of Kyoto, and defeated his opponents. Nobunaga thereupon proceeded to the convent, drove the monks out, and set fire to the buildings. He then returned to Osaka, which surrendered.

Nobunaga had two lieutenants trained by him, in whom he had great confidence. Both were able and brave men. The first was Hideyoshi (hid-ee-yosh-ee). At first this man had no name to boast of, for he was only the son of a poor peasant, and therefore had no right to be a warrior. He began life as a betto (bet-toh) or groom of Nobunaga; but he showed so much skill and courage, that first he was allowed to enter the ranks and afterwards received a small command. In this he proved so successful, that he was again and again promoted, until he was second in command to Nobunaga.

He was very small in size, ill formed in limbs, and altogether made a very poor impression. The redeeming features were his eyes, especially when he smiled; but I must tell you his story in another chapter, after I have given an account of Nobunaga's death.

Hideyoshi was besieging a castle which was defended so stubbornly that Nobunaga went to his assistance. On his way the latter heard that there was a conspiracy in the palace of the capital, and, leaving his troops to continue their march, he went with a small band to Kyoto. When night came on, he sought shelter in a Buddhist convent. In the middle of the night this cloister was surrounded by the clansmen of one of his captains upon whom he had played some practical joke. This captain attacked the convent and set fire to the buildings. When Nobunaga saw that no escape was possible, he ended his life in the samurai fashion; that is, he committed hara-kiri.

THE LORD OF THE GOLDEN WATER GOURDS

IN the last chapter mention was made of the low origin of Hideyoshi, and in a former chapter I told you how the Japanese nobles adopted coats of arms or crests, just as the noble families of Europe did during the Middle Ages. Hideyoshi, of course, had no crest; but when, in 1575, he obtained a command, he adopted a water gourd as his emblem, and added another one for every victory he gained, until the number grew into a large bunch, and he was called The Lord of the Golden Water Gourds.

When Hideyoshi heard of the death of his friend and master Nobunaga, he knew that it was his duty to punish the murderer. But, if for that purpose he should raise the siege, he was quite certain that the rebel chieftains would fall upon his rear, and endanger the situation. His decision, however, was soon made. He informed the besieged of the murder, and frankly confessed that he was about to pursue the man who was responsible for Nobunaga's death. He concluded by saying that he was willing to make peace with them for a time or forever; but if they did not accept his terms then and there, he would soon return with as powerful an army as could be raised in Japan. You will readily understand how those proud chieftains hated the upstart, but they knew also that "the crowned monkey," as they called him on account of his features, was not the man to make idle threats, and that the army of Nobunaga would be ready to join him. They therefore accepted his terms and agreed to serve under him. Reënforced by his former enemies, Hideyoshi now advanced upon Kyoto.

Brave and reckless as he was, the anxiety to reach the capital before Nobunaga's traitor captain could secure a foothold, caused the general to hurry on before his army. About halfway between Hiogo (hee-yoh-goh) and Osaka, he came unexpectedly upon a scouting party of the traitor, and a fight ensued in which he was parted from his guard.

There was a small temple, surrounded by rice fields, which resemble swamps because of the constant irrigation needed in the growing of rice. A narrow path, scarcely wide enough for a horse, led to the temple, and Hideyoshi spurred his horse over it. Near the temple he jumped off, turned his horse on the path, and pricking it with his dirk, sent it galloping back. He then ran into the temple, where he found the priests taking their baths. The bath room in Japan is a large square apartment where all can take their baths at the same time. So Hideyoshi threw off his clothes and jumped in, and when his pursuers searched the temple, they took only a cursory glance at the bathing priests. But now Hideyoshi's guard had come up, and the scouting party was driven off. Hideyoshi put on his clothes and continued his march at the head of his troops.

For twelve days the traitor who had planned to take Nobunaga's place had been master in Kyoto, when Hideyoshi with his army approached the Yodo River. The same battlefield where Japan's fate had been decided when the Minamoto were defeated by the Taira, was to see a new ruler rise to direct her destinies. The traitor's troops were routed, and as he was trying to escape, he was nearly killed with a pitchfork in the hands of a peasant. He ended his life in the usual way, by hara-kiri, but his head was cut off and put on a stake near the place where Nobunaga had fallen. This victory made Hideyoshi master of the situation, and he was not the man to neglect his opportunities.

It was natural enough that the chieftains, who had unwillingly and after repeated struggles submitted to Nobunaga, should object to obey the orders of a man of such humble origin as Hideyoshi. But it was not long before they learned that, willingly or not, the orders issued by the "crowned monkey" must be obeyed. He marched against the chieftains who denied his authority, and after a few decisive battles, convinced them that a strong hand ruled in Kyoto. Then, for the first time in many years, order was restored and Japan began to recover from the long period of misrule and civil war.

Nobunaga had been a general and nothing more. The Lord of the Golden Water Gourds was not only an able general: he was also a crafty politician. In those days the Japanese were very superstitious; in fact, they are so even to this day. I do not mean the few who have traveled in this country or, in Europe, but the great mass of the people. I have told you before that the principal food of the Japanese is rice, and the peasants have the greatest respect for Inari (ee-nah-ree), the god of rice. Wherever you go in Japan, you will see shrines erected to him, sometimes by the roadside near a village, at other times hidden in a beautiful copse of maples or evergreens, or again covered by the leaves of the bamboo, near the fence of a farmyard. The peasants also believe that the fox is the servant of the rice god, and that he can bewitch people. One of Hideyoshi's maidservants took a notion that a fox had bewitched her, and was so convinced of the fact that the other servants began to be afraid of her. The matter was reported to Hideyoshi. He smiled, and said there was a cure for this. He wrote a letter to the god of rice, requesting him to find out which fox had done the deed, and to punish him if he could give no good reasons for his action. The woman, firmly believing that this letter would have the desired effect, was soon cured.

On one of his campaigns, it was necessary to ship a number of horses across an inlet of the sea. The boatmen were afraid. "We don't like to," they said; "the sea god might be angry, and what would become of us then?" Hideyoshi quietly called for pen and paper, and gravely indicted a letter which read as follows:—

HONORABLE MR. SEA GOD:

The horses belonging to the army of the Heaven Child must be transported across this inlet, and I, the unworthy commander of these troops, have engaged the boatmen to perform this work. As they are acting in the service of the Tennô, you will please grant them a safe passage.

This letter was read to the boatmen and then cast into the sea. Satisfied that this would appease the sea god, the boatmen promptly transported the horses.

Hideyoshi had now pacified Japan; that is, the daimio acknowledged him as their master, because they had been made to understand that any disobedience would bring swift and sure punishment. The Lord of the Golden Water Gourds was sure of his army, and he was no niggard in giving land to his faithful captains. From this time, the land really did belong to the daimio, although in theory they held it in fief, that is, as a loan, from the Tennô.

SECOND INVASION OF KOREA

I HAVE told you before how the rich and powerful Buddhist monks opposed Nobunaga. To curtail their influence, Nobunaga showed much favor to the Portuguese missionaries, and the greater part of the island of Kiushiu was converted to Christianity. The missionaries also succeeded on the island of Hondo, and one of the most favored captains of Hideyoshi was a Christian. The Lord of the Golden Water Gourds was indifferent. He did not care whether a Japanese was a Christian or a Buddhist, so long as he obeyed the laws as laid down by him. But now that Japan was pacified, the question arose as to what to do with the large number of soldiers whom his successes had brought to his standard.

These soldiers were samurai, or knights. To them it seemed the greatest disgrace to learn a trade or to earn a living. They were willing to defend their country or their lord, but they demanded to be supported in time of peace, without being compelled to do any work, except to practice with their arms. The country, however, was now too poor to support such a number of men in idleness. Besides this, these samurai were fond of fighting. For some time Hideyoshi kept them quiet by introducing a ceremonious tea drinking, the rules of which were very complicated and caused much study. But he knew that he must give them more serious work, or he would have to face awkward troubles at home.

While considering this question, the thought occurred to him to occupy his troops with the conquest of China. He did not for a moment doubt that they could accomplish it. American boys sometimes use the expression, "It is as easy as falling off a log." Hideyoshi thought the same thing when he said, "It is as easy as rolling up a mat and carrying it off under the arm." When he finally made up his mind, it was decided that Korea should first be captured.

Hideyoshi could not very well assume the title of regent, for that would have offended the whole of the Japanese nobility; but he secured the office of prime minister, which gave him more power than any regent had ever possessed. He could declare war without consulting anybody. Soon it was speedily known that an expedition against Korea was to be made.

When the poor Koreans heard what was in store for them, they did not like it at all. Between the Chinese on one side, and the Japanese on the other, they had a hard time of it. The Chinese had forbidden them to send tribute to Japan, and so they had not sent any for almost a hundred years. This was all very well so long as the Ashikaga regents pretended to rule Japan; but now that there was a man at the head of the government who knew how to make himself obeyed, the Koreans sent several embassies to settle the dispute in a peaceable manner.

But Hideyoshi did not want peace. He had determined to conquer China, and nothing less than that would do. Besides this, he firmly believed that the Japanese had conquered Korea under Empress Jingu, and that it really belonged to Japan. Preparations were therefore made to send a strong army so that this conquest would not occupy too much time, and so that China's turn might come as soon as possible. This took place near the close of the sixteenth century.

But who should command this expedition? Hideyoshi was too well acquainted with the history of Japan to trust one general, who after being successful might declare himself independent; then it would be more difficult to punish him than to conquer the peninsula. To go himself would be exceedingly dangerous, since his absence from Japan might lead to the rebellion of the nobles, who were not over fond of him. At last he decided to divide the expedition into two armies, to be commanded by two of his best officers, who were not only rivals, but hated each other; so that one would act as a check upon the other.

It may be that the introduction of the system of official spies dates from this time. It is a very curious custom, and shows the distrust the samurai have toward each other. It is well worth reading about, and will be explained more fully in another chapter.

When a large fleet had been assembled, Hideyoshi appointed to the command of one army, one of his captains who had become a Christian; whereas the general in charge of the other army hated all the Christians, and especially his rival. Now you might think that these two armies would not be apt to work very well together, and so it proved. At first they carried everything before them. The Koreans were defeated, and Soül (sowl), the capital, was taken. The Japanese acted very brutally wherever they went. But war is always conducted with more or less cruelty, and in those days soldiers thought it their duty to shed as much blood as they could. The king of Korea left his capital and withdrew to Ping-yang on the Tatung (tah-tongue) River, the same place where the Japanese defeated the Chinese in September, 1894. But here also he was followed by his enemy, and. it looked for some time as if Korea would really become a province of Japan. Meanwhile the two Japanese armies acted independently, and the king of Korea sent an embassy to the emperor of China, asking for immediate assistance.

The ruler of this great empire was very well aware that if the Japanese succeeded in conquering Korea, he would have brave and ambitious neighbors who would give him no rest. So he decided at once to help the Koreans. To gain time, he first sent officers to the Japanese to order them to get out of the peninsula on threat of punishment from their master. The Japanese only laughed, and they made it very uncomfortable for these officers. But the emperor of China was now thoroughly alarmed, and, collecting a powerful army, sent it into Korea.

If the two Japanese generals had acted in harmony, there is no doubt that they would have defeated the Chinese. But they did not even help each other, and the consequence was that one army was defeated, and the other was besieged in the capital. The name Japanese had now grown so detested in Korea that the usually gentle people would attack and kill any single Japanese, and it was dangerous for the samurai to walk in the streets, unguarded. At last the Japanese were compelled to treat for peace, and the only trophy which Hideyoshi's troops brought from China was a ghastly heap of ten thousand ears, cut off from the heads of Koreans. A mound was built over them in the form of five tiers, and is still shown in Kyoto as a token of Japanese courage.

Korea has never recovered from this Japanese invasion. Cities and fields were laid waste, and while the Japanese are said to have lost a hundred thousand men, the loss of Korean lives must have been much greater.

When the remnant of Hideyoshi's army returned to Japan, they brought with them a number of skilled Korean workmen, who instructed the Japanese in new and better ways of making porcelain and what is known as Satsuma (sat-soo-mah) ware. That was all the benefit they derived from their expensive expedition.

Chinese ambassadors had arrived in Kyoto, and handed to Hideyoshi a letter in which their emperor offered to make him king of Japan. But the Lord of the Golden Water Gourds was not like the Ashikaga regents. He was furious, tore up the letter, and plainly told the messengers that Japan was an independent country concerning which the Chinese emperor had nothing to say. He would no longer listen to them, but sent them away in disgrace.

Now, though this war was begun and maintained by Hideyoshi, still he had officially retired from public life before the expedition had left, and had been succeeded by his baby son Hideyori (hid-ee-yoh-ree). But so it had been for years in Japan. As soon as a good, strong man was established as the real head of the government, he would resign in favor of some puppet, and from his retirement would wield more power than ever before. Hideyoshi died seven years after he had resigned. He is best known among Japanese boys and girls by the name of Taiko Sama (ti-koh sah-mah), or My Lord Taiko, a name assumed by him when his son became prime minister.

THE THREE HOLLYHOCK LEAVES

AMONG the chieftains of the smaller clans who had joined in opposing Hideyoshi after Nobunaga's death was one whose badge was three hollyhock leaves in a circle. This squire, as he might be called, claimed to be a descendant of the Minamoto. He said that one of the younger sons of Minamoto had, in the twelfth century, adopted the name of Tokugawa (toh-koong-gah'-wah), and that the father of this young squire, himself a warrior of some reputation, had adopted this crest or coat of arms.

Young Hollyhock had served, both under Nobunaga, and under Hideyoshi. When, after Nobunaga's death, he foresaw that the "crowned monkey" would soon be master of Japan, he hastened to make peace with him, and Hideyoshi rewarded him by giving him his sister in marriage and making him governor of the fertile plain around Yedo (yed-doh) Bay. Since the Ashikaga regents, Kamakura had no longer been the capital, and Hollyhock looked around for another place to build a residence for himself. He chose the site where Tokyo (toh-kyoh) now stands, and named it Yedo or Door of the Bay.

So Hollyhock was brother-in-law of the Lord of the Golden Water Gourds, and uncle of Hideyori, who had succeeded his father. But Hideyoshi had but little confidence in the ability of his son, for on his deathbed he appointed his brother-in-law as guardian, and nominated a council to assist him in the government. It soon became evident that Hollyhock would allow no one to dictate to him, or even to interfere with his plans. His opponents in the council took alarm, and, accusing him of plotting, raised a force. A battle was fought in the first year of the seventeenth century, in which Hollyhock was the victor, and from that moment he was the ruler of Japan.

The real name of this most remarkable man was Iyeyasu (ee-yay-yas). He established a new family of regents, and his descendants ruled over Japan for more than two hundred and fifty years, indeed until 1868, when the present emperor was taken from the seclusion in which his family had lived for centuries in the capital, and assumed the duties of government. It was this regent who decided that it would be better for Japan to decline having anything to do with the outside world, and who therefore forbade foreigners to come to, or Japanese to leave, the country. To sum up in a few words, he made of Japan what she was at the time when Commodore Perry steamed up Yedo Bay in his flagship, the Mississippi.

Iyeyasu became the real ruler of Japan in 1600, and his first task was to redivide Japan. The chieftains who had helped him in battle received large additions of territory, which was taken from those who had opposed him.

The title of every chieftain, as I have explained before, was daimio. Some of these lords had very large possessions and were very powerful. Iyeyasu saw that as long as he could keep them divided, and prevent them from plotting together, and especially from obtaining possession of the sacred person of the puppet emperor, the government would continue in his hands and in those of his descendants. To accomplish this, he created a large number of new daimio, from among his most faithful officers, and supplied them with land taken from the great daimio or from property of his former opponents.

He took care that not only the capital, but also every territory, whose lord was not known to be stanch to him, should be completely hemmed in by daimio in whom he could place confidence because their interests were the same as those of the regent, and as he improved the spy system to a standard of excellence unheard of in the history of the world, he was tolerably sure that nothing could pass in any territory within the limits of Japan, that would not be accurately reported in the regent's capital before it could become dangerous to the state or to the regent's interests.

Up to this time there had been no written laws. The control over the people was so absolute, and the supervision so strict, that criminals were few, and punishment was meted out to them in short order. It was a principle of Japanese unwritten law that no prisoner could be executed unless he had confessed, and to obtain the avowal of his crime, torture was resorted to. The judge, in civil as well as in criminal cases, was expected to render a verdict prompted by common sense.

Every daimio had the right to judge in his own territory; but if his people believed themselves in any way oppressed, they had the privilege of an appeal to the regent, who, if the daimio was proved guilty of misgovernment, had power to remove him to another territory or even to condemn him to commit suicide. Japanese books tell of many instances in illustration of this custom.

Iyeyasu knew that the prosperity of the country depended upon the industry and thrift of the masses, and he was firmly resolved to afford them protection. But his sympathies were with the samurai, and he granted them such privileges as to make them really masters of the people.

They were above the law; that is a samurai could not be judged as one who belonged to the common people. But he had a code of honor, the violation of which involved suicide by hara-kiri, or eternal disgrace accompanied by expulsion from his order. The clan, moreover, was held responsible for the good behavior of every samurai belonging to it, and a crime committed by one of them might be punished by a verdict of hara-kiri for several members, especially for those who were in a position to prevent its commission and had neglected to do so.

On the other hand, if a samurai felt himself insulted, he was compelled to wipe off the stain with blood; and if he could not do so without endangering his clan, he had the privilege to become a rônin (roh-neen), or a free lance, who owed allegiance to no one, but acted wholly upon his own responsibility.

This privilege was resorted to especially in cases where the act of a samurai might embroil the clan with the regent's government in Yedo. The samurai was, in such a case, risking his own life, but that was a matter of minor consideration. He had been brought up from earliest youth in the belief that loyalty to the clan was the first and vital principle of the samurai; he had been taught that the sacrifice of his life might be demanded at any time, and that such a death would render him celebrated, not only among the members of his own clan, but wherever the language of Japan was understood. If he read books, the subjects of most of them were incidents in the lives of loyal samurai, generally ending in a ceremonious hara-kiri. If he visited the theater, the same subject was illustrated on the stage. To him death was an incident, to be coveted rather than feared.

The clan itself was or became in time a theocratic republic, that is, a republic of which the daimio, supposed to be a god, was the president; and he could be elected only from the family of the daimio. I have told you before how puppet emperors were made and unmade; how the same fate awaited the regents who succeeded in power; and the clans were naturally governed on the same plan. When Iyeyasu created new daimio out of his best officers, they, of course, ruled their clans in person, but even they were compelled to consult the samurai out of whose ranks they had risen.

The bravest and ablest of these samurai naturally obtained the greatest influence in the clan, and formed a council in which its affairs were deliberated and decided upon. The daimio was then acquainted with their decision, and if he approved, his crest or seal affixed to a document gave it the force of law, and the clan was expected to, and would, abide by it to the death. If the lord of the clan did object to anything approved by his council and could not be brought to reason, another council was held, and if the decision of the first was affirmed, the daimio was respectfully but firmly informed that he must resign. In such a case his heir was raised to the dignity and the former lord withdrew into private life. The honor, dignity and policy of the clan were thus intrusted to the ablest among them, and loyalty was not a personal affair, but one belonging to the clan as a body.

Try to remember this and you will understand how Japan, in a very few years, has made such rapid progress. But now I must tell you some true stories of how the Portuguese succeeded in converting the Japanese to Christianity; why they were expelled from the country; and why Iyeyasu forbade foreigners to come to Japan.

THE DUTCH IN JAPAN

IN the fifty years that had gone by since the Portuguese first landed in Japan, they had made many converts. In Kiushiu alone they baptized more than fifty thousand Japanese and founded fifty churches. The daimio of Arima (ah-ree-mah), Bungo (Boon-goh), and Omura (oh-moo-rah) were among the number who embraced Christianity, although they did not openly favor the new religion.

The trade with Japan was exceedingly valuable to Portugal, for many tons of gold, silver, and copper were exported from Japan every year. The large profit from such a trade made other nations of Europe anxious to obtain a share of it; and because, at that time, the English and the Dutch were the most enterprising, it was natural that one of these should first become a rival of the Portuguese.

The Dutch had fitted out some ships to go trading in the Indian and Pacific oceans, and had engaged an Englishman, Will Adams, to act as their pilot, just as they had taken Henry Hudson to steer one of their ships to America. Here is what Will Adams says of himself:—

"Your worships shall understand that I am a Kentish man, born in a town called Gillingham, two English miles from Rochester, and one mile from Chatham, where the queen's (Elizabeth's) ships do lie; and that, from the age of twelve years, I was brought up in Limehouse, near London, being 'prentice twelve years to one master, Nicholas Diggins, and have served in the place of master and pilot in her majesty's ships, and about eleven or twelve years served the worshipful company of the Barbary merchants, until the Indian traffic from Holland began, in which Indian traffic I was desirous to make a little experience of the small knowledge which God had given me.

"So, in the year of our Lord God 1598, I hired myself for chief pilot of a fleet of five sail of Hollanders, which was made ready by the chief of their Indian Company; the general of this fleet was called Jacques Mayhay, in which ship, being admiral, I was pilot."

The fleet set sail from Holland on the 24th of June, 1598. The ships of those days were small and carried, besides a strong crew to defeat any enemy who might attack them, and the necessary arms, a very heavy cargo, so that there was not much room for provisions or fresh water. Before these vessels had crossed the equator, so many of their crew were sick that they were compelled to seek the nearest land, which was the coast of Guinea, and here many of their men died, among whom was their admiral,—or general, as they called him.

After more than nine months they reached the Straits of Magellan, in April, 1599, "at which time," says honest Will, "the winter came, so that there was much snow: and our men, through cold on the one side and hunger on the other, grew weak." Although there were no charts of the Straits of Magellan at that time, Adams preferred that route to going round Cape Horn; but they were forced to winter there, you can easily imagine under what hardships, and it was the 24th of September before they succeeded in getting into the Pacific.

Here they were caught in a storm which scattered the ships, the Erasmus, of which Adams was the pilot, making for the coast of Chile, where Adams waited twenty-eight days for the other vessels to join him. They, however, were never heard of with the exception of one which they lost sight of again on the 24th of February, 1600. It had been decided that they should make for Japan, for the greater part of their cargo consisted of woolen cloths, "which would not be much accepted in the East Indies because they were hot countries."

"On the 11th of April, 1600," Will Adams continues, "we saw the high land of Japan, near unto Bungo; at which time there were no more than five men of us able to go. The 12th of April we came hard to (close to) Bungo, where many country barks came aboard us, the people whereof we willingly let come, having no force to resist them. And at this place we came to an anchor.

"The people offered us no hurt, but stole all things that they could steal; for which some paid dearly afterward."

The pilot here gives a hard name to the Japanese, but does full justice to the authorities. Theft was and is very severely punished in Japan. But the humbler classes of the people are full of curiosity, and they did not think that they were stealing when they pilfered from the ships. When people go traveling in foreign countries, they will now and then chip off little pieces of monuments or statues, yet they do not consider it stealing; and it was from the same feeling that the Japanese took whatever they could find.

The Portuguese were at that time at war with Holland; but even if this had not been the case, it was not to be expected that they would welcome a rival. You must remember, besides, that they were devout Catholics, who detested the Protestants, and it was chiefly on account of religion that Holland was making war upon Spain and Portugal. You will understand, therefore, that the Portuguese did all they could to give the strangers a bad reputation, and honest pilot Adams says:
—

"The evil report of the Portuguese caused the governor and common people to think ill of us, in such manner that we looked always when we should be set upon crosses, which is the execution in this land for piracy and other crimes. Thus daily more and more the Portugals (Portuguese) incensed the justice and people against us."

But the Japanese acted on the whole very honorably. The daimio sent soldiers on board to see that none of the cargo was stolen; they piloted the ship into a safe harbor, until the regent (Iyeyasu) decided what should be done, and in the meanwhile they obtained permission to land their sick, among whom was the captain, and were given a comfortable house. Iyeyasu, at this time, was at Osaka, and he sent orders that Will Adams and one of the sailors should be brought, before him. The story is told so simply and in such a straightforward manner by him, that I will let him tell it to you in his own words. It will also show you what kind of a man Iyeyasu was:—

"So, taking one man with me, I went to him, taking my leave of our captain, and all the others that were sick, and commending myself into His hands, that had preserved me from so many perils of the sea. I was carried in one of the king's (regent's) galleys to the court at Osaka, about eighty leagues from the place where the ship was. The 12th of May, 1600, I came to the great king's city, who caused me to be brought into the palace, being a wonderful costly house, gilded with gold in abundance.

"Coming before the king (Iyeyasu), he viewed me well, and seemed to be kind and wonderful favorable. He made many signs unto me, some of which I understood, and some I did not. In the end there came one who could speak Portuguese. By him the king demanded of what land I was, and what moved us to come to his land. I showed unto him the name of our country, and that our land had long-sought out the East Indies, and desired friendship with all kings and potentates in way of merchandise, having in our land divers commodities, which these lands had not; and also to buy such merchandise in this land as our country had not.

"Then the great king asked whether our country had wars. I answered him, 'Yea, with the Spaniards and Portugals (Portuguese), being in peace with all other nations.' Further, he asked me in what did I believe. I said, 'In God that made heaven and earth.' He asked me divers other questions of things of religion, and many other things, as what way we came to his country. Having a chart of the whole world with me, I showed him through the Straits of Magelhaens (Magellan); at which he wondered, and thought me to lie.

"Thus, from one thing to another, I abode with him till midnight. And having asked me what merchandise we had in our ship, I showed him samples of all. In the end, he being ready to depart, I desired that we might have trade of merchandise, as the Portugals (Portuguese) had. To which he made me an answer, but what it was I did not understand. So he commanded me to be carried to prison. But two days after he sent for me again, and inquired of the qualities and conditions of our countries, of wars and peace, of beasts and cattle of all sorts, of heaven and the stars. It seemed that he was well content with all mine answers. Nevertheless, I was commanded to prison again; but my lodging was bettered in another place (but I received better lodging in another place).

"So I remained nine-and-thirty days in prison, having no news neither of our ship nor captain, whether he were recovered of his sickness, nor of the rest of the company (crew)."

All this time the Portuguese were trying to induce Iyeyasu to have Adams and his fellow sailors executed, but after considering the question he answered thus, according to Adams:—

"That as yet we had done no hurt or damage to him nor to any of his land, and that therefore it was against reason and justice to put us to death; and if our countries and theirs (Portugal) had wars one with the other, that was no cause that he should put us to death." Adams adds: "The emperor (regent) answering them in this manner, they were quite out of heart that their cruel pretense failed; for the which, God be praised!

"Now, in this time that I was in prison, the ship was commanded to be brought so near to the city, where the emperor was, as she might, the which was done. So the one-and-fortieth day of my imprisonment, the emperor (regent) called me before him again, demanding of me many questions more, which are too long to write. In conclusion he asked me whether I were desirous to go to the ship to see my countrymen. I answered that I would very gladly do it; so he bade me go. Then I departed and was freed from imprisonment. And this was the first news that I had that the ship and company were come to the city.

"Wherefore, with a rejoicing heart, I took a boat and went to our ship, where I found the captain and the rest recovered of their sickness. But at our first meeting aboard we saluted one another with mourning and shedding of tears; for they were informed that I was executed and long since dead."

Everything had been taken out of the ship, but Iyeyasu would have no such robbery. He had the cargo and personal property collected and ordered money to be given to the captain and his crew to procure food and other necessaries. He had, in the meanwhile, returned to Yedo, and ordered the ship to be brought there. The sailors mutinied, demanding all the money, and Iyeyasu refused to allow them to return. They now scattered, each man going where he pleased. They received during life two pounds of rice per day each, and about $20 per month, a liberal allowance, in days when everything was cheap.

But Adams rose in great favor with the regent. He tells us: "So, in process of four or five years, the emperor (Iyeyasu) called me, as he had done divers times before, and would have me to make him a small ship. I answered that I was no carpenter, and had little knowledge thereof. 'Well,' saith he, 'do it so well as you can; if it be not good, it is no matter.' Wherefore at his command I built him a ship, of the burthen of eighty tons, or thereabouts; which ship being made in all proportions as our manner is, he coming aboard to see it, liked it well; by which means I came in more favor with him, so that I came often into his presence, and, from time to time, he gave me many presents. Now being in such grace and favor with the emperor (Iyeyasu), by reason I taught him some points of geometry and the mathematics, with other things, I pleased him so, that what I said could not be contradicted. At which my former enemies, the Portuguese, did greatly wonder, and entreated me to befriend them to the emperor in their business; and so by my means, both Spaniards and Portugals (Portuguese) have received friendship from the emperor, I recompensing their evil unto me with good."

The captain of the Erasmus was at length permitted to return. He carried letters from Adams to England, where the pilot had a wife and two children. Adams hoped that when it was known where he was, some effort would be made to obtain his release, for Iyeyasu found his services too valuable to allow him to return. He received a piece of a land and the revenue of a village for his support. His tomb was discovered about twenty years ago at Hemi (hay-mee), a village on the railroad between Yokohama and Yokosuka (yo-kos'-kah). There is a street in Tokyo, An-jin (an-jeen) Cho,—Pilot Street,—named after him.

PERSECUTIONS OF THE CHRISTIANS

MANY Spanish and Portuguese missionaries came to Japan, and the number of converts was constantly increasing. But the different orders of priesthood began to quarrel among themselves, and the regent of Japan was a man who was decided to maintain peace in his domain. In the year 1597 captains of Portuguese vessels were notified that they must not bring any more priests into the country; but none the less priests continued to come from the Spanish possessions in the Philippine Islands, and some monks, with more zeal than discretion, went to Kyoto, preached in the streets of the capital and even began to build a church there, although this was against the law. Japanese books also mention that in 1596 a Portuguese bishop met on the street one of the highest officers of state going to court. Instead of having his chair stopped, as the law of courtesy required, he not only ordered his bearers to go on, but turned his head aside in contempt when he passed the official's chair. This in itself was a direct insult, and no Japanese will forgive a willful breach of the laws of courtesy. This officer ever afterwards felt a deadly hatred against the Portuguese, and continually reminded the regent of their vanity, pride, and insolence.

In these days, too, the native converts had become overzealous; they insulted the Buddhist priests, broke their images, and even destroyed their temples. Iyeyasu thought that he saw danger to the state in this aggressive way of preaching the Christian religion, and decided to pluck it out, root and branch.

The persecution of the Christians had commenced a year before the death of Hideyoshi. In 1597 twenty six Christians were crucified, most of them being native converts, although a few Portuguese were among the number.

In the year 1609 two Dutch ships arrived in Japan. They had come for the purpose of capturing the Portuguese vessel which sailed once a year from Macao, but they were five or six days late. Their captains went up to Yedo; there they were received by the regent, who was favorably disposed toward them through the efforts of Will Adams. A treaty was made by which they agreed to send one or two vessels a year for the purpose of trading. The first vessel arrived in 1611, and her officers and crew were kindly received and entertained.

Before the Dutch had time to establish any influence, the persecution of Christians broke out with great fury, and it increased a few years later, in 1614, when a great many of the Japanese converts, who would not abjure their faith, and trample on the cross, suffered death by crucifixion. Monks and priests of religious orders were scattered and many fled from the country.

All this time the Portuguese merchants were not interfered with, though captains of vessels were repeatedly notified that they must bring in no more missionaries. But as they still continued to smuggle in priests, a law was made by which they could trade only in the small island of Deshima (day-shee-mah), in the harbor of Nagasaki (nang-ah-sah-kee). If you look on your map you will see that this famous old city is on the west coast of Kiushiu. It has a beautiful harbor.

A Portuguese vessel from Japan, bound for Lisbon, was captured by the Dutch near the Cape of Good Hope, and among the papers of this ship was found a letter from a Japanese Christian, known to Europeans by the name of Captain Moro (moh-roh). This letter was addressed to the king of Portugal. It contained a request for soldiers and ships, which had been promised from Portugal, with the aid of which the captain and his friends hoped to overturn the empire and form a new Christian government. The letter contained also the names of several daimio who had agreed to join the conspiracy. The Dutch lost no time in delivering this letter to the Japanese authorities. Moro was arrested, and although he denied his guilt, his signature and private seal were sufficient to convict him. He was burned alive at the stake, and in the course of that year, 1637, a law was passed that the whole race of the Portuguese, with their mothers, nurses, and all their belongings, should be banished forever. And the same law contained the clauses which secluded Japan from the world until Perry appeared in Yedo Bay.

This law says: "No Japanese ship or boat, or any native of Japan, shall henceforth presume to quit the country, under pain of forfeiture and death; any Japanese returning from a foreign country shall be put to death no nobleman or samurai shall be suffered to purchase anything of a foreigner; any person presuming to bring a letter from abroad, or to return to Japan after he has been banished, shall die, with all his family, and whosoever presumes to intercede for such offenders shall be put to death," etc. It also contained provisions against the Christian religion and the converts, and from that year the persecution of the Christians continued relentlessly.

Several Portuguese left at once; a few remained, hoping that the affair would pass over, but the regent, having determined that they should go, declared them enemies of Japan. They were compelled to leave, and their profitable trade passed into the hands of the Dutch.

The native Christians, cruelly persecuted and oppressed, entered into open rebellion, and this, it appears, was what the government desired. They defended themselves bravely at Shimabara (shee-mah-bah-rah), and the government then appealed to the Dutch for aid.

The chief of the factory, as the trading office was called, upon receiving the regent's orders, left for the doomed town, and after having planted a battery, assaulted it from the shore and from his ship. The Christian Japanese made a strong defense, and the town was blockaded for nearly two months before it was taken; then men, women, and children were slaughtered. The Dutch had received permission to withdraw before this final act.

It is stated in Japanese books that over 40,000 men were killed on both sides before famine rendered the town defenseless, and now the work of stamping out Christianity was continued with the greatest cruelty. A small band, secretly continuing the service, escaped the strict search. They were discovered after the revolution of 1867, and scattered to various parts of Japan, but upon the request of the British minister, they were permitted to return home. Shortly after this, the edicts against Christianity were removed, and now a Japanese may believe what he pleases, provided that he does not doubt the divinity of the emperor and his ancestors.

RESTRICTIONS OF THE DUTCH

IT was partly because the Dutch imported goods which were needed by the Japanese, but also because Iyeyasu saw the necessity of knowing what was passing in the world, that they were permitted to dwell and trade in Japan, under very severe restrictions. The island of Deshima, or Outward Island, in Nagasaki harbor, was assigned to them as a residence and trading post, but it was little better than a prison. A small stone bridge connected the town with the island. This bridge was closed by a gate, and near it was a guard-house occupied by policemen and soldiers, who prevented the Dutch from leaving the island without express permission, and the Japanese from entering unless they were officially employed. All those who entered or left were closely searched. No foreign servants were allowed, and the natives could serve their foreign masters only between sunrise and sunset, as they were not allowed to pass the night on the island.

The Dutch lived in houses built by some enterprising Nagasaki people, who rented them at a very high price. They were allowed to furnish them as they pleased, and to obtain their furniture from Batavia or have it made by Japanese workmen. They were not permitted to handle their own money, probably from fear that they might bribe the officers; but the government appointed a paymaster who settled all the bills, and when a ship arrived, the cargo was taken by Japanese agents who sold it, and with the money thus received, settled the account of the paymaster, and purchased the goods which the general agent desired to send back.

The number of Hollanders allowed to reside on Deshima was eleven: a general agent, who was held responsible for the good behavior of the other inmates; a warehouse master, who attended to the storing and delivery of the goods; a secretary or bookkeeper; a physician; five clerks; and two warehousemen. Wives or daughters were under no circumstances permitted to land or reside on the island.

The paymaster, interpreters, servants, and all those connected with the foreigners were provided with a ticket which they were obliged to show to the guard whenever they passed through the gate. These persons, before they entered upon their duty were compelled to sign, with their own blood, an oath promising to enter into no friendship with the Dutch; to give them no information whatever about the history, religion, laws, manners, or language of Japan. Except for this the

Hollanders would have been glad to while away the time by studying the customs and manners of the country; but the scant information which they managed to extract, now and then, by bribery, was not very reliable.

At first the general agent was required to go to Yedo once a year to pay his respects to the regent, and to offer the presents agreed upon when the Dutch were permitted to reside in Japan. But the expense of the journey was so great that these presents were soon sent through Japanese, and the general agent himself went only once in four years. These journeys were always begun in February, that month with March, April, and May being the most pleasant for traveling. It took a long time to make the necessary preparations, for the Japanese are very fond of ceremonies, and the omission of even one would have been deemed a serious insult.

The party of Hollanders going to the capital usually consisted of the general agent, his secretary, and the physician, together with a large number of native officials and servants. Most of the journey was made on land, and each of the Hollanders, as well as each of the native officials, was carried in a norimono (noh-ree'-moh-noh), a sort of sedan chair, with windows closed with bamboo curtains and a roof like that of a house. All these norimono required bearers. Besides these there were the carriers of the presents, the boxes containing clothing, cooking apparatus, chairs, etc., and the numerous cooks and body servants of the Dutch and the officials. Altogether there were not less than two hundred persons, and although they were frequently entertained by the daimio through whose territories they passed, the expense connected with such a trip was very heavy.

Because it will convey to you a good idea of what Japan was under the government of Iyeyasu and his successors, I shall give you an account of such a journey made by Dr. von Siebold, who lived in Deshima as physician of the trading post, and who succeeded in learning much concerning Japan.

During the journey across the island of Kiushiu, the Dutch were entertained by the various daimio. As they approached the territory of one of these lords, they were met by a detachment of samurai who welcomed them in name of the daimio and escorted them through his domain. They left their norimono at Kokura (koh-koo-rah) to wait for their return, and here they went on board a vessel prepared for them. They landed every night on one of the thousand islands with which the Inland Sea is dotted, and if the wind was unfavorable, they were sometimes detained several days. But they were obliged to reach Yedo within a given time, although a liberal allowance was made for unavoidable delays. The doctor found that several guidebooks existed in which the distances, charges at inns, price of bearers and of ferries, were accurately given.

The roads in Japan are uniformly good, and are kept scrupulously clean; frequently they are bordered with trees, and the views are everywhere beautiful. One of the sights which struck the travelers was the number of stalls where straw shoes for horses and oxen are sold. The people counted the distances by the number of horseshoes that were required. They do this still in the interior where there are as yet no railroads. The Dutch were much interested, too, in the farmyards which they passed on their way. At one place, Dr. von Siebold visited a Buddhist temple, where he found no idols excepting Buddha, and the priests there were allowed to eat meat. At another place he found a camphor tree that had been mentioned by another traveler from Deshima in 1691. He measured it and found it about fifty feet in circumference. It was still standing in 1826, and was green and healthy.

When they passed through the territory of the daimio of Hizen (hee-zen), the Hollanders were invited to bathe in the daimio's own bath, and found it exceedingly clean; the water, although clear as crystal, was made to run through fine sieves, so that not a particle of dirt could pass in. Another daimio offered them the use of his own private rooms in his country seat. From such courtesies received everywhere along the road it was evident that the Japanese did not object to having foreigners live in their country.

When they left Kiushiu, they sent the heavy baggage ahead to rejoin them when they should land at the main island of Hondo. They had a prosperous voyage across, though on the previous journey, the party had been detained a long time by storms and head winds. The Japanese sailors, to induce the sea god to give them favorable weather, threw overboard a small barrel of sake (sah-kay)—that is, brandy made from rice—and a number of copper coins. The money sank, but the barrel floated and was found by some poor fishermen. What do you think these people did with it? Instead of keeping it for themselves, or selling it, they carried it to a temple, for they knew that it was intended for a god, and not for them.

When the party landed in Hondo, they found other norimono waiting for them, and continued their journey overland. They rested for a day or two at Osaka, but were not allowed to go out to see anything. Here, as in every city where they stopped, they were secretly visited by Japanese who wanted to learn something, the greatest number of these visitors being physicians or their patients. Here, too, the general agent ordered such goods as were to be manufactured before his return.

It took a day and a half to cover the distance between Osaka and Kyoto; now it is done by railroad in less than one hour. In Kyoto the travelers rested again, and were watched more closely than at any other place. Still they received a very large number of secret visitors, and here the doctor must have found out that the Tennô was the real ruler of Japan.

And now they entered upon the longest part of their overland journey, where they frequently met some of the daimio, returning from Yedo with a numerous band of samurai. But there was no disorder, nor were the strangers ever insulted; on the contrary, good will and courtesy were shown everywhere.

The road they were now traveling, being used by all the daimio of the south, was strongly guarded. Iyeyasu and his successors had made a law by which all the daimio of the empire were compelled to dwell half the time in Yedo, and when they were absent in their territory, their wives and children were held as hostages in the regent's capital. No one could pass the two guard posts on the road without a special passport, and the officers were exceedingly strict in guarding against the smuggling through of women, probably from fear that the wife of some powerful daimio might leave the capital in secret. Unless personally known to the guard, travelers had to submit to a strict scrutiny, so that no woman could pass in man's clothing. For if a female should pass through without a special permit, the guard knew that death would be his fate.

Here is an instance showing how strictly this law was observed, and how the guard who was responsible escaped detection:—

A poor business man of Yedo was obliged to go to a town on this road. He was a widower with two children, a boy and a girl, and he could not afford to pay for their board during his absence; so he was compelled to take them with him. He had not enough influence to obtain a passport for his daughter, so he dressed her as a boy, and succeeded in passing the guard in the Hakone Mountains. But a little further on, he was overtaken by a man who knew him and his family, and who, seeing the girl in boy's clothing, had no difficulty in understanding the situation. He asked the father for money, and the latter gave him as much as he could spare. The man, however, demanded more, and when the father refused, a quarrel ensued. The man thereupon went back to the guardhouse to betray the father.

The guards were anything but pleased at the man's report. If it turned out to be true, and the facts were published, they would be put to death. But the officer in charge saw a way out of the danger. He sent a messenger with a little boy, to overtake the travelers. They were found at a tea house, taking some refreshments, and the messenger took the father aside, and told him what had happened. "Now," said he, "some officers are going to follow you to inspect the children; if they find the girl, you will all be punished. But you must hide your daughter and take this little boy; and when the officers see that both children are boys, they will let you go, and you can travel on with your own children. If the man who informed upon you says anything, draw your sword and kill him. The officers will not interfere."

In the meanwhile the chief officer of the guard had detailed some of his men to go with the informer to overtake the children, but these men were privately instructed not to hurry, so that the messenger might have time to execute his errand. When they arrived, they surrounded the house and seized the two children. They appeared well pleased to find that they were both boys. The informer, however, insisted that there was some trickery in this, and the father, drawing his sword, cut off the man's head; then the father, exchanging the boy for his daughter, proceeded safely on his way.

A VISIT TO THE REGENT

THE travelers at last approached Yedo forty-eight days after leaving Deshima—a journey which is now made by steamer in two and a half days. As the party came near the gates of the city, they were met by a detachment of samurai who were to act as escort. The Hollanders crossed the city and entered the precincts of the castle, where they were lodged in a house especially prepared for them. Here, in the capital, they were held in even more rigid seclusion than in Nagasaki; but here, also, they were visited by many prominent Japanese, among whom was the daimio of Mito (mee-toh), the brother of the regent. Uniform kindness was shown to them. A great fire procured for them more than usual liberty. As these fires are very common in Japan, even to-day, I shall give the description in the words of one of the travelers:—

"At ten o'clock in the morning of the twenty-second of April, we heard that a fire had broken out in the town, at the distance of about two leagues from our quarters. We took no heed of the news, so common are fires at Yedo—a fine night never passing without one. As they are less frequent during rain, a lowering evening is a subject for mutual congratulation to the people in Yedo. The flames came nearer and nearer; and at about three o'clock in the afternoon, a high wind driving the sparks toward our neighborhood, four different houses around were soon in flames. Two hours before this occurred, we had been sufficiently alarmed to begin packing; so that now, when the danger had become imminent, we were prepared to make our escape.

"On coming into the street, we saw everything blazing about us. To run with the flames before the wind appeared very dangerous; so, taking an oblique direction, we ran through a street that was already burning, and thus reached an open field beyond the conflagration. The place was set thick with the flags of princes (daimio), whose palaces were already consumed, and who had escaped thither with their wives and children. We followed their example, and appropriated a spot to ourselves by setting up a small Dutch flag used in crossing rivers. We had now a full view of the fire, and never did I see anything so terrible. The horrors of this sea of flame were enhanced by the heartrending cries and lamentations of fleeing women and children.

"Here we were for the moment safe, but had no home. The governor of Nagasaki, then resident at Yedo, had been dismissed; and the house of his successor, appointed that very day, was already in ashes. We had quarters assigned to us in the house of the other governor,—then resident at Nagasaki,—which stands quite at the other side of the town. Thither we were led at half past ten in the evening, and were received and all our wants supplied in the most friendly manner."

The next day the travelers received a visit from their former host. "He told us that thirty-seven palaces of princes (daimio) had been destroyed, and that about twelve hundred persons (including a little daughter of the daimio of Awa (ah-wah)) were either burned to death or drowned. This last misfortune was caused by the breaking down of the celebrated bridge Nihon bashi (nee-hon bash-ee), under the weight of the flying multitude. Those in the rear, unconscious of the accident, and wild to escape the flames, drove those in front forward into the water."

And now I shall give you an account of the visit paid by the Hollanders to the regent. As the same ceremonies were always observed, I shall give the account of one of the general agents. He says:—

"A sort of full dress is ordered for the occasion. That of the general agent is composed of velvet; the doctor's and the secretary's are of cloth trimmed with gold or silver lace, or embroidered with gold or silver. All three wear cloaks, that of the general agent being of velvet, the others of black satin; but these are not put on till the men reach the interior of the palace. The general agent alone enjoys the privilege of having his sword borne behind him in a black velvet bag, no other foreigner in Japan being suffered even to retain his side arms.

"On the appointed day, the 28th of the third Japanese month (which then corresponded to the third of May), we repaired in state to the palace, at six o'clock in the morning, that we might be there before the arrival of the state councilors. We were carried in our norimonos into the castle, and to the gate of the palace, where even princes are obliged to alight, except three, who, being princes of the blood, are brought as far as the gate, opposite to the guard of a hundred men. To this guard we proceeded on foot, and there awaited the coming of the councilors of state. We were desired to sit on benches covered with red hangings, and were offered tea and the materials for smoking. Here we saw the governor of Nagasaki, and one of the chief spies or general commissioners for strangers, who, after congratulating us upon our prospect of immediate happiness in approaching the emperor (regent), left for the palace.

"Then came the commandant of the guard to visit the general agent—and here it is necessary to stand rigidly upon one's rank. The commandant required that I should come down from the inner room, which is held the most honorable, into the first or outer room, because his inferior rank did not authorize him to enter the inner room. I, on my side, asserted the impossibility of leaving the upper place assigned me. The commandant then advanced; but he paused at the distance of two mats (about twelve feet), and thence saluted me. By thus resolutely maintaining my place (which must always be done in Japan when one is right), I insured the observance of old customs, the restoration of which—if through good nature one ever gives way—is exceedingly difficult.

"When all the state councilors had arrived, we were invited to cross the other courts and enter the palace, where we were received by persons who, but for their shaven heads, might be compared to European pages. They conducted us to a waiting room, where we sat down on the floor, in a reclining posture, and covered our feet with our cloaks—to show one's feet being considered in Japan an act of gross rudeness. After remaining here some time, the governor of Nagasaki and the commissioner for foreigners led me into the anteroom, where I was desired to perfect myself in the part I had to act, as the governor would pay the penalty of any imperfection. I was then led back to the waiting hall. Not long afterwards I accompanied the governor to the reception hall, from which we saw several grandees returning.

"I was led along a wooden corridor to the hall of a hundred mats, so named from its being carpeted with a hundred mats, each six feet by three. They are made of straw, are about two inches thick, and over them are laid others of finer texture, ornamentally bordered; such mats are used in Japan to cover every handsome sitting room. There we left the chief interpreter, and, with the governor of Nagasaki, I was now ushered into the audience hall, where I saw the presents arranged on my left hand. Here we found the emperor (so the Dutch considered the regent), whose dress differed in no respect from that of his subjects. I paid my compliments in the precise form in which the princes of the realm pay theirs, while one of the state councilors announced me by the shout of Capitan Horanda! (Holland Chief). Hereupon the governor of Nagasaki, who stood a step or two behind me, pulled me by the cloak in token that the audience was over. The whole ceremony does not occupy one minute."

It is entirely true that the general agents paid their respects in the same manner as the daimio paid theirs, and as every Japanese salutes his equal or his superior in rank. Still it was somewhat humiliating to men of their race. Here is a more detailed description of the ceremony, given by a most trustworthy eyewitness:—

"As soon," he says, "as the general agent entered the hall of audience, they cried out 'Horanda Capitan,' which was the signal for him to draw near and make his obeisances. Accordingly, he crawled on his hands and knees to a place shown him, between the presents ranged in due order on one side, and the place where the emperor (regent) sat on the other; and there, kneeling, he bowed his forehead quite down to the ground, and so crawled backward like a crab, without uttering a single word. So mean and short a thing is the audience we have of this mighty monarch."

A SHREWD JUDGE

A MONEY LENDER of Osaka at one time missed a sum of money amounting to over three thousand dollars. Aghast at this discovery, and almost in despair at his great loss, he tried to remember the names of his customers and visitors since he had counted his hoard, but could attach suspicion to no one. He now began to watch his servants and at last felt convinced that one of them, if not the actual thief, was aware of what had become of his gold. This servant, Tsuji, (tsoo-jee) was taken by the money lender into his private room, and accused of the theft, which, however, he emphatically denied. His master tried to obtain a clue to the whereabouts of the lost money, first by promises of pardon and even of reward, and, when these proved of no avail, by threats of speedy punishment. But it was all in vain. Tsuji protested that he was innocent, and had no knowledge whatever of his master's gold. The money lender then had him arrested for the theft.

Osaka, the second city of the empire in population, is now and has been for many centuries the wealthiest city of Japan. It is situated in the south-central part of the island of Hondo, accessible to junks, which, on account of the many canals intersecting the city, can load and unload in almost any quarter. Being close to the Inland Sea, and only a short distance from Kiushiu, and Shikoku, it almost controls the trade of these three islands. To protect the commercial interests of its enterprising merchants, the regents in Yedo took care to send able and good men as governors, who were at the same time judges in civil and criminal cases. At the time we are speaking of, the governor judge was Matsura (mah-tsoo-rah), a good, able, and shrewd, man.

Tsuji was brought before this judge and examined by him. After hearing all the circumstances, the judge was inclined to believe in the man's guilt, but in answer to the questions put to him, the servant replied simply: "I do not know!" or "I did not do it!" At last the judge threatened to have him tortured, but Tsuji said: "You may do your worst; but no amount of torture will make me confess a crime of which I am not guilty." The quiet, firm way in which the prisoner uttered these words and his fearless bearing had their effect upon the judge. Nevertheless he gave a signal, and Tsuji was led to prison.

The governor now sent for the money lender and his other servants, and examined one after the other. Each one declared that no one but Tsuji could have stolen the money. But when asked for proofs, they were obliged to confess that they had none.

The money lender was very angry with his former servant, and implored the judge to have him put to death. Matsura sat for some time in deep thought. At last he seemed to make up his mind. He ordered the other servants to be brought before him and asked master and servants if they were ready to declare in writing and over their hand and seal that Tsuji was guilty of the theft, and demand his execution. All agreed to this. "Very well," said the judge, "let each of you sign this!" And he gave them a paper on which was written:—

"Tsuji, servant of our master, has robbed him of five thousand dollars. This we attest hereby, and demand that he be punished with death, as a warning to others. We, the kinsmen and servants of our master, affix to this our signatures and seals."

After they had signed this paper and put their seals to it, they returned it to the judge, who said: "This paper relieves me of all responsibility. Is it your desire that Tsuji be put to death?" "It is," they replied. "So be it!" said Matsura. The money lender then withdrew with his servants, after thanking the judge for complying with his request.

Not long afterwards, a robber was arrested in the act of stealing, and brought before Judge Matsura, who ordered him to be put to torture. This man was a daring criminal and he confessed stealing the money lender's hoard, besides many other crimes. There was no doubt of his guilt, since he entered into details of how he had secured and spent this money. As soon as this confession had been written down and signed, Matsura sent for the money lender and his servants, and, addressing the former, said sternly:—

"You accused Tsuji of stealing, without proof of his guilt. You demanded the death of an innocent man, and I, who should have insisted upon proofs before granting your request, condemned him. The dead cannot be brought back, but justice can and must be done. You, your wife, kindred, and servants, shall die. And I, who am also guilty, will commit hara-kiri."

The money lender and his servants, knowing the character of the judge, felt that there was no escape. They were overwhelmed with despair, wrung their hands, wept, and begged for mercy. But the judge sternly refused to listen to their piteous cries. The officers of the court also interceded with the judge for his own life, telling him that he had done no wrong by pronouncing sentence after receiving the written statement of the plaintiff. But the judge replied only: "No, if these men are guilty, I cannot be innocent."

When all were convinced that nothing could move the judge, he spoke again to the despairing money lender:

"You know now how hard it is to die, but you had no pity when you demanded the blood of a man who had served you honestly and well. I should not be worthy of the trust placed in me if I had listened to your demand, and had condemned the prisoner without convincing proof. Tsuji is alive, and therefore your life shall be spared. But for the long imprisonment he has undergone, and the agony and suspense which he has suffered, you shall compensate him. My judgment is that you shall pay him the amount you accused him of stealing; and that it be made known in public that he is innocent of all crime."

The money lender, overjoyed at having his own life saved, gladly agreed to this. Tsuji was brought into court and informed that his innocence was established and that he would be a rich man. Japanese writers tell this story with pride, as showing that, even if they had no written laws, their judges were quite able to see that justice was done.

TOSA'S REVENGE

IYEYASU had given his granddaughter in marriage to Hideyori, the son and heir of his late chief and brother-in-law Hideyoshi, but this did not prevent him from making himself regent. Many of the great daimio saw that they would have even less power under the new regent than they had possessed under the "Lord of the Golden Water Gourds," and so they conspired against Iyeyasu under pretense of defending Hideyori's rights. Among these lords was the daimio of Tosa (toh-sah). He followed the fortunes of Iyeyasu's grandson, and when his party was defeated, fell into the hands of the victor. Iyeyasu had him put in prison, and treated him as a common criminal. But Japanese of the warrior class are not easily daunted, and Tosa persisted in upbraiding his conqueror until Iyeyasu ordered his hands cut off, which was the greatest disgrace he could inflict upon him. So far from humbling Tosa, this only served to exasperate him; and at last he was beheaded by order of the angry regent, and his estate was confiscated.

Tosa left a son, nine years old. Young as he was, this child understood the disgrace which his father had suffered, and even at that early age, thought of nothing but revenge. But Iyeyasu had taken proper precaution, and he, and his heirs after him, were too firmly established and too powerful to be easily disturbed. Years passed by, the boy grew to manhood, and was noted for his skill and strength in arms. He appeared to have completely forgotten the cause and circumstances of his father's death, but this attitude was only assumed to confirm the fancied security of his enemy. Still he had no opportunity to satisfy his revenge until the great-grandson of Iyeyasu, named Iyemitsu (ee-yay-meets), succeeded as regent. The lawful heir of Tosa was then appointed commander of the pikemen of the new regent's uncle, and thought that the moment had arrived to gratify his sole object in life.

By some means he discovered that the regent's uncle had no great affection for the new ruler, and when he sounded this uncle's former tutor, a man of humble birth but of great ability, he found ready sympathy. His plan was to destroy the whole race of Iyeyasu and to divide the empire between himself and the tutor. Strange as it seems, it appears that the regent's uncle knew and approved of the conspiracy, although he was probably not aware of the fate in store for him if the plans of the conspirators were crowned with success.

As I have told you in another chapter, the spy system had been brought to a rare degree of perfection, and although Tosa had kept his secret hidden in his heart for almost fifty years, the approach of success seems to have rendered him more careless. An incautious remark caused suspicion, and careful investigations led to the disclosure of his scheme. Orders were given to arrest him and the tutor, but, in order that the names of the other conspirators might be discovered, it was decided to take him by surprise.

One evening when Tosa was at home, happy in the thought of the near approach of the longed-for revenge, an alarm of fire was sounded near his door. Without any suspicion of trickery he ran out to see if there was any immediate danger; and was suddenly surrounded and attacked: He defended himself bravely, cutting down two of his assailants, but was at length overpowered by numbers and taken prisoner. His wife had heard the noise and suspected the cause. While the fight was going on, she went to the place where her husband kept his papers, and burned them. When the officers entered to search for the list of the conspirators' names, they could not find it. Tosa's wife, for this act, is held in the highest esteem, even by the Japanese of to-day, and the greatest flattery that can be bestowed upon a woman of that country is to compare her to Tosa's wife.

The regent now gave orders to arrest Tosa's intimate friends. The tutor escaped capture by committing hara-kiri. Two of the prisoners, upon being examined, at once confessed their share in the conspiracy, but sternly refused to reveal the names of their friends.

These two men, together with Tosa, were then given over to torture. I shall not describe in detail the shocking ordeal through which they passed; it would have shamed even the horrible ingenuity of the North American Indian. But the fortitude of the Japanese samurai character was such that when they were laid upon hot ashes, after being plastered all over with wet clay, one of the prisoners said: "I have had a long journey, and this warming is good for my health; it will supple my joints, and render my limbs more active." Other and more dreadful tortures were applied, and Tosa, urged by the judge to reveal his accomplices, to avoid further suffering, replied scornfully: "Scarcely had I completed my ninth year when I resolved to avenge my father and seize the throne. My courage thou canst no more shake than a wall of iron. I defy thy ingenuity! Invent new tortures; my fortitude is proof against them all!"

Since no information could be obtained from them, the prisoners were condemned to death, and the day for the execution was appointed. According to Japanese law of those days the wife and mother of Tosa, with five other women, were also to suffer the death penalty. The condemned numbered thirty-four, and, headed by Tosa, they were led in procession through the streets of Yedo. When they had reached the execution grounds, a well-dressed man whose two gold-hilted swords announced his rank, made his way through the crowd, and approached the minister of justice whose duty it was to be present at capital punishment. Making the customary salutation to the representative of the law, he said: "I am a friend of Tosa, and of the tutor. As I live at a great distance, I have but lately heard that their conspiracy has been discovered, and I came at once to Yedo. I remained in hiding, hoping that the regent would pardon Tosa. But now, as he is about to die, I come to bid him farewell, and, if necessary, to die with him."

"You are a worthy man," replied the minister, "and I wish that every one were like you. It is not necessary that I should request the regent to grant your wish. Go and bid farewell to your friend Tosa."

The two friends were allowed to communicate without being interfered with. Tosa thanked his friend for coming to see him once more, at so great a risk. His friend took a sad farewell and in parting said: "Our body in this world resembles a magnificent flower, which, blooming at early dawn, fades and dies as soon as the sun has risen. But after death we shall be in a better world, where we may without interruption enjoy each other's society." Having said this, he left, after thanking the minister for his kindness.

The prisoners were then fastened to separate crosses, and there killed by the sword. Tosa's wife suffered death with no less fortitude than her husband.

I, have told you this story to give you an idea of Japanese manners, in the days of Iyeyasu and his successors. But it was only in certain cases that men of the class to which Tosa and his friends belonged, were publicly executed. Treason against the regent was one of these. He knew that the power wielded by him in Yedo was not lawfully his, and that any noble, with sufficient forces, could cause his downfall and make himself regent. Public execution involved not only disgrace, but also loss of all property. Hara-kiri prevented both, while it elevated the name and family of the suicide. The samurai, while showing no sign of dissatisfaction when one of their number was condemned to kill himself, were apt to murmur when one was publicly disgraced. And no man, whatever his rank and influence in Japan, could afford to arraign this most powerful class against him.

Tosa's wife was not examined when her husband's papers were missed; for in Japan a woman was legally incapable of giving testimony, and even if the names of the conspirators had been wrung from her under torture, the government could not have made use of her confession, because it was given by a woman. She was condemned to death, not because she had burned important papers, but because she belonged to Tosa. If there had been any children, they also would have suffered the same penalty, regardless of age or sex. Such was the law of Japan until within recent years.

Before I close this chapter, you will like to hear what became of Tosa's brave friend who visited him just before his death. He stopped to witness the execution, and, when all was over, he returned once more to the minister, to whom he presented his two swords, saying: "I am indebted to you for the last conversation with my lost friend; and now I beg of you that you will report me to the regent, for I wish to die like Tosa."

"I will not do so," replied the minister, "for you deserve a better fate than that. You bravely came forward to bid him farewell, while others remained in hiding, anxious only to save their worthless lives."

The regent's uncle also was suspected, and so grave was the suspicion against him that he was in danger of being arrested. And now occurred one of those instances of loyalty of which we read so often in Japanese books. The secretary of this daimio came forward and declared that he, and he only, knew of the conspiracy, and that his lord was guiltless. And to prove his statement, he resorted to the usual method,—he committed hara-kiri, and thereby saved his master's life and estate.

A WIFE'S NOBLE ACT

BEFORE Iyeyasu died, he gave large territories to his sons, and made provision in case one of his successors died without leaving a male heir, that he should adopt an heir from one of the three high families descended from him. Such a case happened when a regent lost his only son by an accident. But this man, who possessed none of the excellent qualities of his ancestor, determined to adopt as son and heir a boy, who was the child of a favorite, and of inferior birth.

Imagine the scandal this project caused in a court where high birth and rank were regarded with the utmost respect and reverence. The prime minister sought his master, and plainly told him that the act he meditated would rouse not only the daimio unfavorable to the regent's family, but also those of the blood of Iyeyasu, and their friends, and that indeed this step would probably cause the downfall of his house. As the regent would not yield to argument, the prime minister took the unheard-of step of consulting the regent's wife. This lady was the daughter of a Tennô, and was proud and high-spirited. She listened quietly to the prime minister's remarks, and when she was fully informed of the danger involved in her husband's purpose, bade the alarmed official be of good cheer, saying she would undertake to avert the threatened peril. She declined, however, to inform him concerning her plans.

Time passed on, and finally the regent appointed the day when the adoption should take place. The court was aghast, for the daughter of the Heaven Child had given no sign of her proposed action. At, last only one day was left, when the regent's wife, long neglected by her wicked husband, sent him a message requesting that he would condescend to partake of sake in her apartments. He consented, and in due time made his appearance. She received him as if nothing had happened, and, according to Japanese customs, served him humbly. While he was drinking, she withdrew for a few moments to her private room, and there wrote and forwarded a note to the prime minister, in which she summoned him to the palace. Then, after placing in her girdle a beautiful dagger, she returned to the room occupied by her husband.

The regent, was in high spirits, and willingly granted her request for a private audience, whereupon she dismissed the attendants.

"My lord," she said, "is all-powerful, and can easily grant the request his humble slave would submit."

"And what is this request?" asked the regent, thinking that it might concern some departure from established palace rules.

"Now let my lord deign to promise me," she insisted; but the regent would not pledge himself until he knew her wishes. Seeing that her husband could not be induced to give the desired promise, she plainly stated the facts:—

"I am informed that you have decided to adopt a young friend as your heir. My honored lord, has it occurred to you that this step would arouse the fury of your most powerful kinsmen, and that they would prefer to see the empire ruined rather than submit to this public insult and disgrace? I implore you, therefore, to abandon your purpose."

"What!" exclaimed the regent, in surprise and wrath. "Since when does a woman presume to speak about affairs of state! What madness is this? Think you that I who take advice from no man, will be influenced by a woman's foolish notions? I forbid you to speak to me again, nor shall I ever honor you with another visit."

The regent rose to go; but his wife, detaining him by the sleeve, and for a moment casting aside her accustomed submission to her husband's will, protested:

"Reflect, O my lord and master! Deign to remember that naught but anxiety for your welfare causes me to make this request. If you carry out your plan, rebellion will soon destroy your house. May I not live to see that day!"

"No more of this!" exclaimed the regent, his anger now aroused to the highest pitch. His wife saw that nothing could move him from the resolution he had taken; so, seizing a moment when he stood facing her, she plunged her dagger twice into his breast. Her hand was steady, and the regent fell dead at his wife's feet.

She knelt by his side, and implored him to forgive her for having employed the only means within her power to secure the regency to the house of Iyeyasu, of which, since her marriage, she was an insignificant member. "Do not think, my lord and master, that I care to live, now that I have slain you. I have raised my hand against you and know the punishment." She bared her breast, and stabbed herself with the dagger, still red with her, husband's blood.

The prime minister had received the letter, and hurried to the palace. But a great deal of time was consumed before a high official could leave the house. First, the norimono must be prepared, and the bearers called together. The bodyguard must assemble and be ready to surround the master's conveyance. And finally the heralds, loudly shouting: "Down on your knees! Hita ni iru!" (shta nee-eeru), must have a fair start, so that common passers-by may show proper reverence to their lord.

Thus it happened that when the regent's palace was finally reached, and the minister was conducted to the apartments of the regent's wife, he found the two corpses, life being wholly extinct. After gazing upon the sight before him, the minister exclaimed: "Japan is saved, and by a woman! But for her daring act, to-morrow's sun would have witnessed riot and rebellion and the downfall of an illustrious race!"

In her letter to the minister the woman, knowing that she was facing death, had calmly given instructions as to the measures to be taken if anything should happen to the regent. The prime minister, full of admiration for the dead woman's courage and devotion, obeyed her orders, and the legal heir was proclaimed regent. The prime minister received an ample reward, and the disappointed candidate was raised to the rank of daimio, and obtained a grant of land. Japanese writers express great admiration for the heroic conduct of this regent's wife.

In the laws made by Iyeyasu, Japanese women did not have many privileges. A great many girls were taught to read and write, but it was only that they might be the more impressed with the one all-absorbing duty of women,—obedience. To render, when unmarried, blind, immediate obedience to parents, or, if these were dead, to the head of the family; to enter into marriage without being at all consulted, and after marriage to transfer this obedience to husband and family, this was the fate of a Japanese girl. When Mutsuhito (who became emperor in 1867) assumed the government, many changes were made, and it seemed for some time as if Japan would adopt our customs. But, so far as women are concerned, the Japanese have returned to their old modes of thinking, and they are now of the opinion that their treatment of a woman is the best.

THE FORTY-SEVEN RÔNIN

I MUST now tell you a story of which the Japanese are very fond. Boys and girls never weary of reading it, and whenever it is announced that this play is to be acted in a theater, the house is sure to be filled. Every foreigner coming to Japan hears about it, and his guide or interpreter is always anxious to show him the mean-looking burying ground where the heroes of this story are laid to rest.

But to you and to me this tale is of importance chiefly because it gives a fair idea of the character of a samurai, and shows why the people of Japan place so much trust in the members of that class.

A certain regent was expecting a visit from his brother, who was on his way to open a new shrine to the war god, and two daimio were appointed to receive the visitor, and to see that he was entertained according to his rank. Treason excepted, there is no greater crime than to be ignorant of the proper ceremonies due a visitor, and in order that no mistake might be made, an officer of the court was appointed to instruct the two daimio. Of course, both were anxious to learn, but the court officer being avaricious, the chief secretary of one of the daimio bribed him to take more pains with his master. This the court officer did, and he frequently made insulting remarks to his second pupil, while complimenting the first upon his natural aptitude, and flattering him in other ways.

At first the offended daimio thought that it was really to correct his awkwardness that these remarks were made. But when every successive day brought new insults and hidden taunts, he began to suspect that they were intentional, and he decided to punish the offender. He communicated this intention to his chief secretary, who perceived at once what was amiss. Begging his master to have patience for a few days, he hastily collected as much gold as he could, and in the evening paid a visit to the instructor. He began with praising his entertainer's skill and knowledge of ceremonies, and deplored his own ignorance, declaring that it was due to this that he had omitted to offer him a slight present as a token of respect from his lord, but that he wished to repair this grave error by tendering his humble gift. The court noble made a gracious reply; his eyes glistened as he felt the weight of the gold, and the faithful secretary felt assured that his lord would thereafter have no cause to complain of rudeness.

The daimio was wholly ignorant of the step taken by his secretary. All night he brooded over the insults that he had received, and they grew in number and importance as he recalled what had passed since he first entered the court noble's room. When he prepared to go to his daily ordeal, it was with the firm purpose that his instructor should die, if he dared act in his usual manner.

When, however, the daimio entered the room assigned to the exercises, the court noble bowed low before him, and protested that hitherto he had misapprehended his lordship's faculty; and with other soft words attempted to curry favor with a man who could afford such presents. The daimio took this unwonted politeness as a more refined insult, and, drawing his sword, rushed upon his tormentor. Others interfered, and prevented him from inflicting more than a slight wound.

But drawing a sword within the palace was an offense scarcely less in degree than high treason, and the punishment was severe. The daimio was condemned to commit hara-kiri, and his castle and lands were taken by the regent. His samurai might take service under another clan or turn rônin; that is, free lances.

When their lord had committed suicide, his secretary called together the samurai of the clan, and gave to each one his share of the cash in the treasury. Some of the older clansmen, furious at the insult to their master and the clan, proposed to follow their lord's example, because any resistance to the regent's decree would be hopeless. But the young samurai were in favor of resisting to death the surrender of the castle. Some, indeed, received their share, and quietly withdrew, without taking further part in the discussion. Only one, who had occupied the same rank as the secretary, abused him for dividing the money evenly, stating that his superior rank entitled him to a greater amount. But he, too, disappeared, and shortly afterwards offered his services to the same court noble whose avarice had caused his master's death.

When these samurai, more intent upon their own future than upon avenging the honor of the clan, had left, only forty-seven remained. The secretary, satisfied that they were loyal, now divulged his plan. He advised them to surrender the castle quietly to the officers of the regent, and to disperse in such manner that they could be easily brought together. He expressed the hope that their object in life would be to avenge in the blood of the court noble the insults and misfortunes of the clan; and that therefore they would take no service, but live on the money received from the treasury. All signed an agreement to this effect with their blood. The widow of the daimio moved to Yedo, trusting the management of her affairs to the devoted secretary.

This faithful samurai took his wife and family to a village near Kyoto, where he rented a small cottage. He knew that his loyalty to his master was known, and that the court noble would take sufficient precautions to insure his safety, so long as he feared the vengeance of the clan. Already the court noble had doubled the number of his samurai, and much as he loved money, he did not hesitate to pay liberally for spies to keep him informed of the doings of such members of the hostile clan as he feared most. He was confirmed in his opinion that a plot existed, because no resistance had been offered when the regent's officers appeared to take possession of the castle; and it was for the purpose of counter-scheming that he had engaged the former councilor of the dead daimio.

The secretary now set about lulling his enemy into security, and while in secret he remained a good husband and father, he began to visit tea houses and to lead, apparently, a very frivolous life. His best friends thought his mind had been unsettled by the misfortunes that had befallen his clan.

Of course, the spies employed by the guilty court noble kept their master informed of the conduct of the man suspected by him, and as month after month passed by, he began to think that, after all, his expensive precautions might be unnecessary. But the secretary's character was well known by his former friend and fellow-clansman, who proposed to his new master to let him proceed with one of his confidential samurai to the village inhabited by his enemy, and to find out if this conduct did not conceal a deep-laid scheme of revenge.

The court noble assented to this plan, and the two men arrived in the village. It did not take them long to discover the name and location of the tea house where the secretary was wont to spend much of his time. They decided upon surprising him there. Near the place, they heard shouts of laughter from the waitresses, and when they entered the tea house, they saw the secretary blindfolded, playing a game of blindman's buff with the girls. The two spies asked for a room; they were informed that they could have one on the next floor, but that the ground floor had been engaged by the secretary. They ordered some sake, and settled down to watch.

Presently they saw four men approaching and recognized three of them as free lances, former samurai of the proscribed clan. The fourth man was a common soldier, who wished to be admitted into the band of avengers. They had entered the inn, when the blind-folded secretary, trying to catch the girls, fell against one of his fellow-clansmen: "You are caught!" cried the secretary, "and now as forfeit you shall drink a cup of sake!"

The free lance shook him off. "What do you mean by acting in this way?" he said. "I am your former clansman, and here are two of our friends. I must speak with you."

"What about? asked the secretary, in an indifferent tone; then, turning to the waitresses, he added: "I don't think I want to play any more."

"We want to know when you propose going to Yedo!" said the spokesman of the four.

"Yedo!" repeated the secretary. "Yedo! Oh, that's a long way off! What are you talking about?"

The rônin were furious. They would have killed their former leader, had not the soldier interfered. But the man was really anxious to join the conspirators, and modestly made his request. The secretary answered: "What is the use of revenge? If we succeed, we shall die; and if we fail, we must die also. What is the good of it all? What is the use of taking medicine, when one is going to be beheaded the next day?"

Still the soldier repeated his request; but the secretary, stretching himself upon the mats, yawned, turned round, and soon appeared to be fast asleep. The samurai left in despair.

THE FORTY-SEVEN RÔNIN (CONTINUED)

THE spies were watching. They had not been able to discover any plot, although they had overheard every word spoken in the rooms below. The night passed, and dawn was commencing, when they fancied they heard cautious footsteps; a door was opened, some one entered, and a few words passed in a whisper. Then the footsteps were again audible, but soon grew fainter, and silence once more prevailed.

It was the secretary's son who had aroused their attention, the young man having come to seek his father. When he saw that they were alone, he cautiously took out a letter. "It is from our lord's widow," he said. "The court noble is going to leave Yedo. If we do not kill him now, the opportunity may be lost forever."

"Go back," whispered the secretary, "and when it is dark, send me a covered litter."

The secretary lay down, but did not sleep. He thought long and deeply, and when daylight appeared, he arose and took the letter. At this moment his former friend, the spy, entered the room, and the secretary quickly hid the letter in his breast, not, however, without having been observed. Both watched each other intently, while professing to be glad to meet again.

"What good wind brings you here?" cried' the secretary. "It seems an age since we parted, and our foreheads are not any the smoother for the lapse of time. This is a good occasion to drive wrinkles away!"

"Why, Sir Secretary," the spy replied. "Is this the way you set about to avenge our lord?"

"Avenge! avenge! what nonsense is this?"

Both called for sake and breakfast. The traitor, when he saw the secretary eat fish, stood aghast. He believed that the spirit of his unavenged lord might have wandered into an animal, and took care to partake only of vegetable food. The secretary readily understood what was passing in his mind, and to confirm the impression he had made, said with feigned contempt:—

"Who has heard that our lord has turned into a fish? Bah! A chicken would be even better eating. Let me order one!" and he went out to see about it. This act may be considered the most heroic of all those performed by this loyal samurai. It filled him with loathing, for he was as superstitious as his opponent. But he wanted to convince the spy of his own worthlessness, and chose the most efficacious means.

When the secretary had left the room, the spy's comrade entered. They agreed that nothing was to be feared from a man so utterly ruined in principle, as was the secretary, and having finished their mission, they decided to depart.

The spies entered their curtained litter, but the secretary's former friend passed out on the other side, and hid under the floor of the porch, whispering to his companion, "I am not yet wholly satisfied. Go on your way. I mean to discover what was in that letter."

When he saw The litter depart, the secretary came out on the porch, and proceeded to open the letter his son had brought. It evidently contained matters of importance, for the reader was plunged in deep thought as he continued to unfold it. It was so long that part of it reached down to the ground, and the spy succeeded in drawing it through the cracks in the floor. What he read confirmed his suspicion. He was now convinced that a conspiracy existed, and that the secretary was the leader. The question was: how could he obtain proof that would convince his employer; this was all the more necessary since his fellow-spy was satisfied that there was no conspiracy. He decided to tear off part of the letter.

Now it happened that one of the waitresses had come out on the upper porch to listen to some strolling players. Seeing the secretary's letter, and curious to know what it might contain, she seized her metal hand mirror, to obtain a reflection. But the mirror fell, and the secretary saw her. He called out to her, "Come down, my girl. I have taken a fancy to you and shall purchase your release from this place."

The girl, pleased at leaving this service, was coming down, when the soldier who had applied for admission among the conspirators reappeared. He was the girl's brother. He had heard the secretary's offer, and while the latter entered the tea house to pay his bill, the soldier asked his sister what it all meant. She answered that she had read part of the letter, and told him the contents. "Woman's curiosity!" he exclaimed. "The secretary will kill you to make sure of your silence." "Let him do so!" she answered. "If my death will assist him, he is welcome to take my life." The secretary, who had missed part of his letter, now returned. He overheard what was said, and told the soldier that no harm would befall his sister, but that he wished to keep her safe until the affair was over.

A search was at once begun for the culprit who had torn off part of the letter; and the spy was found and dragged from his hiding place. With the assistance of the soldier, he was bound and gagged, taken to the river, and drowned. His death relieved the secretary of all immediate anxiety.

What were the contents of the letter that had caused all this trouble? The daimio's widow, who had kept herself informed of all the court noble's actions, wrote that her enemy had dismissed most of the guards he had hired, as he was about to leave Yedo. With the small number of samurai at present in his yashiki (yash-kee), or residence, it would be comparatively easy to finish the affair. She urged immediate action.

In a city, not far from Kyoto, lived a merchant who had been agent to the clan; that is, he had sold the rice paid as taxes, and purchased whatever was necessary. This man shared the feelings of the loyal samurai at the misfortunes of the clan, and freely offered his means to help the conspiracy, since he, as a simple citizen, could not devote his life to the cause. His offer was accepted.

The secretary designed a model after which forty-seven sets of armor were made, so that the conspirators could recognize each other in a night attack. The swords and other weapons were stored with the merchant, and so that no gossip might betray what was passing in his house, his wife was sent, for the time being, to her father's home. The merchant agreed to have two well-equipped junks ready to carry the band to Yedo, when the time for the final act should arrive.

Now before the unfortunate episode that ended in the suicide of the daimio and the dissolution of the clan, the secretary's son had been betrothed to the daughter of the man who with his timely presents had bought the court noble's good will. This man and his family had heard of their old friend's sad downfall, and for some time the matter of the marriage had been allowed to drop. But father and daughter had too great a liking for the secretary's son to abandon the project; so, to please his friend, the father had procured a plan of the court noble's house and grounds. He now sent his wife and daughter to the secretary's home, he himself following at a short distance.

The two ladies arrived and were hospitably received by the secretary's wife; but when they mentioned that they had come to confer about the marriage, the hostess grew cold and haughty. "Why did your husband first bribe that wretched court noble," she said; "why did he interfere when my lord was going to kill him? Bring me the head of your husband, and then I may listen to your proposal."

Meanwhile her husband, disguised as a beggar, had arrived and overheard this cruel demand. He had expected a refusal, but this undeserved hatred made him lose his temper. "Here is my head; take it!" he said, entering and throwing off his disguise. "I have heard that your husband is not only a rônin, but also a tramp and a madman, and should not be surprised if the son is like the father. Let them take my head if they can."

The wife of the secretary was almost beside herself at this insult. Seizing a spear from a rack, she made a thrust at him with all her strength, but the samurai caught the weapon and took it from her. To prevent the furious woman from doing mischief, he brought her to the ground and held her down. Just at this moment the door opened, and the secretary entered with his son. The young man, thinking his mother in danger, without waiting for an explanation, picked up the spear, and ran the visitor through the body.

Every one was aghast at the turn of affairs. But the visitor, who felt that the wound was mortal, recollected the purpose of his visit, and gathering all his strength, explained his object. "Let my desire be granted," he concluded, "and I shall die happy. Surely you will not make my journey vain."

In reply the secretary opened the sliding doors into the garden. There, playing the madman, he had made two tombs of snow. He pointed toward these, and the visitor understood that they were for father and son, who were to die before the snow could melt. His wife then said:—

"You understand now why I demanded your husband's head. It was not to insult you; but the court noble must die, and my husband and son will be compelled to commit suicide. Why should my son marry on the brink of death?"

"And yet I insist," replied the dying visitor. "Take this paper; it contains a list of the gifts that my daughter will bring to her husband."

He produced the paper and gave it to the son, who opened it listlessly. But no sooner had he cast his eyes over it, than his face grew animated; and after examining it closely, he cried: "This is no list of gifts, but the greatest of boons. It is the plan of the court noble's residence, with walls, gates, barracks, garden, complete!" And he passed it to his father.

"Thanks, my old friend," said the secretary. "This is, indeed, the best gift we could receive, since it removes the last difficulty. Nothing can now prevent the punishment of our enemy."

"Show me the plan!" gasped the visitor. "See! here is the water gate, and here the main gate. Force an entrance at these two points. You will have no difficulty in making your way to the private apartments, while at the same time you can prevent escape or rescue. And now, before I die, let the marriage take place."

"Very well," replied the secretary. "But I must go at once to arrange for boats, and to collect our men." So, taking a dignified leave of his wife, and bidding farewell to his visitors, he told his son to join him the next day, and left, after offering a brief prayer to Buddha for his friend.

With wife and daughter kneeling beside him, the stanch old samurai was dying. He bore his pain without flinching, and when the lifeless body lay stretched on the floor, the features were in calm repose. The women began the prayers for the dead, while the wife of the secretary thought with pride of her own husband who was so earnestly bent upon preparing his own shroud.

The secretary had hurried to the house of the agent, and found that everything was in readiness. The merchant's wife had not yet returned from her visit, and her father was highly displeased, and considered his daughter divorced. Still the merchant refused to allow her to return, fearing that an unguarded word might betray the cause to which he was devoted.

The evening before the day set for the sailing of the conspirators had arrived. About midnight the agent was aroused by loud and repeated knocking at his door; and when he opened it, six samurai, armed and dressed as city guards, rushed in. He was at once seized and placed under arrest; and the officer in command charged him with conspiring against the life of the court noble.

"We have evidence against you which cannot be denied," said the officer. "We have seized this box which came from your house. Confess at once, and give the names of the other conspirators, or we will put you to torture."

The box was, indeed, full of weapons and chain armor, and had been sent that day on board the ship that was to carry the secretary and his men to Yedo. "Well, thought the poor agent, "all is lost, though through no fault of mine. Yet they shall not discover anything from me. I can die but once; and I will die in an honorable cause." With a sudden effort he threw off his guards, and putting his knees upon the box, dared them do their worst.

"Fool!" said the officer. "What good would it do us to kill you? But we shall find the means to loosen your tongue." At a signal to one of his men, the agent's little one-year-old son was seized and handed to the officer, who pretended to prepare to cut the child's throat. Whatever may have been his feelings, the agent gave no sign of submission.

"Now," said the officer sternly, "we know that this box contains armor and weapons for the secretary and his band of conspirators, and that it came from your house. Confess at once, or first this child shall die and then you shall follow him."

"All I can tell you," replied the agent, "is that I deal in arms as well as in other things. Is that a crime for which an honest man can be put to death? If it is, you must begin with me, and now." So saying, he made a rush for the officers.

"Stop!" thundered the secretary, throwing off his disguise. He now explained that some of the conspirators had expressed fear that the agent, who knew everything connected with the expedition, might betray them at the eleventh hour; and their leader, to make sure, had resorted to this disguise to put the agent to the test. He, as well as all the rônin, apologized for their distrust and openly expressed their admiration for the courage and loyalty of the agent. The secretary willingly accepted an invitation to partake of refreshments, and with two of his men remained, while the others returned on board.

The agent's wife, urged by her father to consider herself divorced, and to accept another husband whom he had chosen for her, had not been able to sleep that night; and, anxious to see her husband and child, she had quietly left the house. Reaching her home while the agent was entertaining his guests, she induced the servant to admit her. Her husband, hearing her voice, left the room and commanded her to return to her father, but he could not explain why he wished her to do so. The merchant was aware that his father-in-law could compel his daughter to marry again,—because when a man sends his wife to her father to stay, it means that he divorces her. Hence although she obeyed his orders to leave the house, she would not go away from the door.

The secretary and his two companions could not help overhearing what was passing, and they appreciated the agent's difficulty. The leader whispered some instructions to them, and they left the house at the back, and passing to the front, met the wife as she came out of the door. They seized the frightened woman, unfastened her hair, cut it off, and, laughing, ran away with it.

They returned by the way they had come, while the wife's outcries brought the agent to the front door. He bade the woman enter and laid his perplexities before his guests. The secretary handed him his wife's tresses, saying that there would be no danger now of any suitors, but that she had better enter a convent for a while, so that her hair might have time to grow. This was agreed upon, and the samurai then took their leave. "I wish," said the secretary in parting, "that you were a samurai; you would then be able to join us, and I am sure not one would be braver. But you shall hear from us long before your wife's hair has grown, so your separation need not be long."

The two junks with the conspirators on board set sail, and in due time arrived in Yedo.

THE FORTY-SEVEN RÔNIN (CONCLUDED)

ON a narrow strip of land extending into the bay, with yashiki residences of other nobles on both sides, was the house of the court noble for whose murder such deep plans had been laid. A dark night had been set apart for the attack, which was to be made according to the directions of the man who had furnished the plan of the grounds.

The appointed time arrived; it was dark and the ground was white with snow. The son, in command of half the band, was to scale the wall near the front gate, while the secretary, with the other half, would enter by the water gate. The party at the front gate were in position and listened impatiently for the signal that the water gate had been forced. After waiting for a long time, two of them cautiously scaled the wall and dropped down on the other side. They heard the watchman's rattle, as he was making his rounds, and when he passed near the spot where they lay concealed, they sprang upon him, gagged and secured him. They forced him to continue his rounds, and to rattle at stated intervals, that nothing unusual might arouse suspicion. At last the signal was heard. Dark forms rushed to the front gate, opened it, and admitted the son with his men, shouting the battle cry agreed upon. The guards and servants, running hither and thither without order or supervision, were cut down by the sharp swords of the avengers. Now they approached the house. In a few minutes the tightly closed shutters were unfastened, and the victorious samurai searched the rooms for their intended victim.

Seated on a stool in the garden, the secretary directed the movements of his men. But the noise had aroused the inmates of the adjacent residences, and men bearing lanterns and torches appeared upon the neighboring roofs, their bearers inquiring into the cause of this disturbance. The secretary with all politeness informed them of the feud against the court noble, adding that there was no danger of fire, so that their residences would not be damaged. His object was vengeance only; but if they were inclined to make their neighbor's cause their own, he was ready to receive them. Satisfied with this explanation, and fully sympathizing with the cause of the disturbers, the uninvited spectators withdrew.

The avenging party was now in possession of the place, but its owner, the object of their vengeance, was not to be found. It looked, indeed, as if he had effected his escape, and the secretary, after detailing men to guard the gates, commenced a systematic search. The residence was ransacked in every nook and corner; but neither there nor in the grounds could be found any trace of the fugitive. In searching the shed used for storing charcoal, a person was found hiding, and being dragged out, was recognized as the missing noble. He was led to the secretary, who, bowing in recognition of the captive's rank, briefly reminded him of the misfortunes he had caused the clan and its lord, and requested him to commit hara-kiri that the soul of the dead daimio might be appeased by having the noble's head placed upon his tomb.

"So be it," was the reply; "my head shall be at your disposal." Then he drew his dagger as if to use it upon himself. But, suddenly rising to his feet, he struck furiously at the secretary. The latter, however, was on his guard and caught his now desperate foe by the wrist. After a brief struggle, the noble lay writhing on the ground. "Do with him as you please!" exclaimed the secretary; and the next instant the swords of the samurai were buried in the body of their enemy.

"O happy hour!" one cried, as he withdrew his sword "O blessed event! For this we have left parents, wives, and children, and lived as homeless outcasts. For this we have refused to take honorable service, that we might be free to wreak vengeance upon our destroyer. Could we live three thousand years, never again might we hope to meet with such good fortune!"

Then the head was cut off, washed, and reverently set upon a temporary altar where the dead daimio's emblem had been placed by the secretary. The samurai then burned incense, and called upon the soul of their lord to approve of the act to which they had devoted their lives. It was now broad daylight, and the city was ringing with their deed. They formed in procession, and, passing before the residence of a high noble, they were invited to enter, and partake of some refreshments. They did so, and were highly applauded for their loyalty. Then proceeding to their lord's tomb, they placed their enemy's head upon it, and committed hara-kiri to escape punishment by the regent.

There is no story told in Japanese books that can give a better idea of the spirit animating a samurai. It is founded upon facts, and explains many circumstances that are almost inconceivable to us. The rule that without progress, persons as well as nations must decay and perish, was defied by Japan. For more than two hundred and fifty years that country was kept stationary. Such a condition would have produced retrogression anywhere else, but it was this spirit of the samurai that saved the country. This sturdy, proud, self-reliant spirit, suffering no superiority, acknowledging no master, impatient of restraint, was stirred to the utmost when, notwithstanding undeniable valor, the samurai suffered defeat from strangers,—inferiors in their opinion, since they were not samurai, nor even Japanese.

Dissembling their real feelings as did the secretary in the story, they set about learning the secret of these strangers' strength. They began to study our arts and methods, with that set purpose which commands success. They introduced our habits first indiscriminately, to discard after closer acquaintance such as might prove harmful to Japan. Self-interest was never considered. When wealth was requisite for their purpose, they would have such wealth, not as an aim in itself, but as an incident to promote their schemes. They have transferred their loyalty from clan to country, and from hollyhock or gentian to the imperial chrysanthemum. What must be the future of a country, guided by such a spirit?

VARIOUS ATTEMPTS TO TRADE WITH JAPAN

WHEN the Hollanders received permission to remain in Japan for the purpose of trading, the English were granted the same privilege; but as they found no profit in it, they at length withdrew. When Charles II. was king, an effort was made to return, but when the Japanese heard that the king was married to a Portuguese princess, they haughtily refused their consent.

Years passed by, and Japan was left undisturbed. If a ship in distress came to their coast, the Japanese would relieve the wants of the crew, and dismiss them. They acted, indeed, in a very humane and kind manner, so long as they were satisfied that it was accident and not purpose, which had led the strangers to their shores. The government, however, was determined to carry out the policy of Iyeyasu and to keep the country in seclusion as long as possible.

The first ship to break through this barrier was the Eliza, Captain Stewart, of New York, near the end of the eighteenth century. Holland was at war with England, and, to avoid capture by British cruisers, engaged neutral vessels to carry merchandise. The Eliza, bearing the Dutch flag, arrived at Nagasaki, and great was the consternation of the officials when they found that no one of these supposed Hollanders understood Dutch. It took some time to make the governor understand that these seamen were not English, although they spoke that language. But even when he did realize the difference between an American and an Englishman, it was with much hesitation that he consented to consider the Americans even as carriers. But at last consent was given, since the war rendered this substitution unavoidable.

The Eliza returned the next year, again engaged by the Dutch. When she was loaded with camphor and copper, she set sail in the evening, but struck upon a rock, filled, and sank. The crew succeeded in getting off in the boats and safely reached the shore, and the question now arose as to how to raise the ship and her valuable cargo.

At first it was decided to employ Japanese divers to bring up the copper; but the camphor had melted, and the gases caused the death of two men. Other attempts to raise the ship followed, but all proved fruitless. When all were at a loss what to do, a fisherman came forward and offered to raise the ship if his expenses were paid. At first he was laughed at; but when the Americans saw his confidence, they agreed to let him try.

He began his work by fastening to both sides of the vessel fifteen boats, connecting them by means of props and stays. When there happened to be unusually high water, he came himself in a junk which he fastened in the same manner to the stern of the sunken vessel. When the water was at the highest point, sail was set on all the boats. The heavily loaded vessel was lifted, she cleared the rocks, and was towed to a spot on the shore where she could easily be unloaded and repaired. The man's expenses were paid, and he was handsomely rewarded, while a neighboring daimio gave him the right to wear two swords, which was similar to knighting him.

It seems that, while this accident kept Captain Stewart at Nagasaki, he conceived the idea of entering into commercial relations with the Japanese, independent of the Dutch. When his vessel had been repaired and her cargo was again on board, he sailed, but encountered a storm which dismantled him, and once more he returned to Nagasaki. At last he departed, and returned the following year, but in another vessel. He stated that the Eliza had been wrecked, so that he had not reached Batavia; that he had lost the cargo, but that a friend in Manilla had furnished him with the means to purchase and load the brig, and that he had come to pay his bill for repairs of the Eliza, for which purpose he offered his cargo for sale.

The general agent of the Dutch listened quietly to this story, and turned the goods in the usual manner over to the Japanese. Now Captain Stewart had stated that nothing had been saved of the cargo of the Eliza, and when several articles that had been shipped on her had been identified among the cargo of the brig, Captain Stewart was arrested and sent to Batavia to be tried for the loss of the Eliza's cargo.

While the investigation was going on, the prisoner made his escape, but in 1803 he entered Nagasaki Bay in another vessel and under the American flag, and boldly requested permission to trade and to supply himself with fresh water and oil. The first request was at once denied, but he was given what he asked for without charge, and was then compelled to leave. The captain after this probably abandoned his purpose; at all events, he was not heard of again in Japanese waters.

Another attempt to open friendly intercourse with Japan was made by Russia. A Japanese vessel had been wrecked off the coast of Siberia, and Empress Catherine II sent home the members of the crew who had been saved. Laxman, captain of the Catherine, which had been chartered for this purpose, entered Hakodate (hah-koh-dah-tay), on the island of Hokkaido (huh-ki-doh), and told the authorities the object of his visit, at the same time requesting that arrangements might be made to establish trade. He was courteously received, but was warned in writing:—

1. That the Japanese law condemned to imprisonment for life every foreigner landing in any part of the empire, except Nagasaki. The government would, however, overlook the offense (on account of his ignorance of these laws, and because of the Russians' kindness to Japanese subjects), on condition that Laxman would promise that he and his countrymen would leave immediately, and would never again approach any part of the coast except the port of Nagasaki.

2. That the Japanese government thanked the Russians for the care taken of its subjects; but that they might leave them or take them back as they pleased, because the government considered all men to belong to the country where they were cast by their destiny and where their lives had been protected. Laxman and his crew had been treated with the greatest civility. Before his departure, he was provided, without charge, with everything he wanted, and finally dismissed with presents.

The troubles arising from the French Revolution caused a cessation of further efforts. But in 1803, Emperor Alexander sent his chamberlain Resanoff as ambassador to the emperor of Japan. Resanoff was not the man to engage in the difficult task before him. First he was insolent and overbearing, and then submitted tamely when the Japanese confined him in a narrow inclosure, resembling a bamboo cage, on the beach at Nagasaki. After some time he was informed that the Japanese government had no desire that Russian ships should enter any port of Japan, and was dismissed unceremoniously. Resanoff returned to Kamchatka, and applied to the captains of two small armed vessels, to procure him satisfaction. Had he sought this at Nagasaki, he might have impressed the Japanese; but instead of this he attacked some of the Kurile (koo-reel) Islands, killed and captured the defenseless inhabitants, and burned their villages. Resanoff died on his way to St. Petersburg.

The Russians had begun to colonize some of the northern Kurile Islands, and in 1811 Captain Golownin (go-lof-neen) was dispatched in the Diana to make a survey of this group. Some of his crew were in danger of being captured when they landed on one of the islands, but Golownin explained that he had come only to take in wood and water; that the act of the two Russian captains had been one of piracy and that they had been punished by the government. This satisfied the Japanese officers, and the Russians received a letter to the commandant of another fortress on the same island, where there was more facility to procure what was needed.

A RUSSIAN CAPTIVE

GOLOWNIN, instead of going where directed, continued his survey, and when he really did need water and other necessaries, he proceeded to one of the more southern islands of the same group, and communicated with the Japanese commandant. This officer pretended to be satisfied until Golownin deemed himself safe; when, having landed without escort, he, his officers, and boat's crew were overpowered and taken prisoners.

First the Russians were tightly bound with small cords; they were rendered so helpless that they had to be fed like infants, since they could not use their hands; the cords by which their legs were fastened had only enough play to enable the men to walk. A soldier held the end of each man's cord, and in this manner they were driven overland, or piled together in boats when transportation by water was necessary.

They were well taken care of, so far as food and drink were concerned, and when they were too tired to walk, their guards willingly carried them. So too, when the people of the villages through which they passed offered refreshments, the prisoners were always allowed to partake, and it seemed to afford their guards pleasure, if they appeared to enjoy these gifts. At the same time the guards would not loosen the prisoners' cords, even though they cut into the flesh and caused intense suffering; but at night the wounds were carefully dressed. At last the Russians received an explanation of the odd mixture of cruelty and kindness with which they were treated. It appeared that the guards had been charged to convey the prisoners alive to Hakodate, and were afraid that one of them might commit suicide from despair at being a prisoner. If this had happened, or if one of the Russians had effected his escape, there would have been no inquiry: the guard in charge would simply have been found guilty, condemned to death, and executed. The kindness shown to the prisoners was, therefore, genuine good nature, while the apparently unnecessary severity was a precaution for the protection of the guards themselves.

After a month, Hakodate was reached. The arrival of the Russians must have been expected, for both sides of the road were crowded with men, women, and children. All behaved in a well-bred manner. "I paid special attention," says Golownin, "to their expressions, and failed to observe an angry look, or a sign of hatred toward us, and there was not the least attempt to insult us by laughing or mockery."

The Russians were taken to a long wooden building surrounded by bamboo palisades. There was a hallway with wooden cages or cells on each side, about six feet square and provided with two small windows with iron gratings, admitting light and air; the floor was covered with mats, and a wooden bench was all the furniture. Each prisoner was put into one of these cells. Through the night, watchmen made the rounds, rattling now and then to announce that they were on guard. In the morning the Russians received water with which to wash themselves, and a Japanese physician came to inquire into the condition of their health.

On the third day they were conducted, under a strong guard, to the house of the governor. Here tea and tobacco were offered them, and they were asked a number of questions, the answers being taken down in writing.

"Has Russia changed her religion?" was one of the unexpected questions.

"Certainly not."

"Why do you wear your hair cut short and without powder, when Laxman, who was here a few years ago, wore a long pigtail and thick hair covered with flour?"

"Fashions change, but they have nothing to do with religion."

This answer the Japanese could not understand, but the interrogation continued.

"Why did you carry off wood and rice, when you landed, without the consent of the owners?"

"We left in exchange other articles, fully equal in value."

"Does Russian law allow you to take anything without the owner's consent, if you leave other articles of equal value?"

"It does not. But if a man takes what is absolutely necessary for his existence, and substitutes full value, he cannot be considered guilty."

"Ah, our laws are different. A man must sooner die of hunger than touch, without the consent of the owner, a single grain of rice which does not belong to him."

When the Russians had been fifty days in Hakodate, they were taken to Matsumai (mah-tsoo-mi), where the governor of the island resided. Here they were again examined, but more minutely. There was a great improvement in their treatment, although they were still confined as before. The weather being extremely cold, they were well provided with warm clothing, and a physician visited them twice a day. If any one was ill, a second doctor would come to attend him.

At last the Russians were removed from their prison to a residence surrounded with strong palisades, and were permitted to walk through the town, accompanied by a guard. They now resolved to escape. After having burrowed under the palisades, one night in April, they crept out, one by one, and, favored by darkness, struck across the country toward the sea, directing their course to the north, and ascending hills covered with snow. Hiding by day, they, for eight nights, wandered through thickets or scrambled among rocks and precipices, at great risk to their necks or limbs.

At length they reached a village on the shore and found two boats, but these were hauled up on the beach, and, weak and famishing as the Russians were, they could not launch them. A little farther on they saw a boat afloat, and near it a tent. One of the famishing sailors thrust his hand into the tent, but instead of finding something eatable, he grasped the head of a Japanese who was sleeping within. The fellow roared out, and the Russians, fearing that the noise would alarm the villagers, hastened back to the hills.

On the next morning, when they were helpless from exhaustion, they found themselves surrounded by soldiers, who came upon them very quietly, bound their arms behind their backs, and led them to a house, where they refreshed them with sake, boiled rice, radishes, and tea. The Russians had been regularly tracked, day by day. Golownin suspected that the old fear about suicide had prevented the Japanese from seizing them sooner. They were marched back to Matsumai, and safely lodged in the castle. The governor showed no anger at this escapade: he merely told Golownin that his plan was ill contrived, and that if he had succeeded the governor himself and other Japanese would have answered for the escape with their lives.

The Russians were soon sent from the castle to a new prison, and put into separate cages. But, at last, when the second year of their captivity was well advanced, they were restored to liberty, and sent off to their own country.

At the time of his capture, the officers of Golownin's ship, the Diana, had attempted to get near enough in shore to be able to use the small cannon with which the ship was armed, but they were prevented by the shallow water. For three days they cruised near the place of the capture, and finally landed near a village, where they left some linen and other articles of which the captives might be in need. Then they returned as fast as possible to the seat of the Russian government on the Pacific coast.

One of the captains of the Russian navy left at once for St. Petersburg to lay the case before the emperor. But at that time Russia was engaged in war with France, and it was some time before Emperor Alexander ordered the Diana to return to Japan. Captain Rikord was appointed to take command. When he sailed, he carried with him seven Japanese who had been shipwrecked on the coast, thinking that he might effect an exchange. But when he reached Japan, he found that he could not enter into communication with the shore, since the Japanese declined to take notice of him. At one place, indeed, they fired upon his vessel.

Under these circumstances, Captain Rikord decided to capture a Japanese vessel, but when he did so, the crew jumped overboard and escaped, and he gained nothing. Soon after this, he captured a large native junk, and although some of the men threw themselves overboard, the captain, a lady passenger, and several of the crew were captured. Most of the sailors were set free, and allowed to proceed with their vessel; but as the season was too far advanced for further efforts, the Diana returned to Kamchatka with her prisoners. There they were well treated, and the captain passed most of his time in studying the Russian language.

The Diana returned to the Japanese coast in the spring, but it was June before she reached the island of Hokkaido. No one would communicate with her; indeed, it seemed as if the coast had been deserted. Captain Rikord now called the Japanese captain and explained to him what he wished him to do. The Japanese stoutly declined to follow his instructions, adding that, if Rikord persisted, he would first kill the Russian and then himself.

By his own desire, the Japanese captain was then put ashore, and made his way to the house of the governor. He took with him a statement signed by the Russian governor of Kamchatka, that the outrage committed in the Kurile Islands had been severely condemned by the government. This document he handed to the governor, stating that, from his own experience, the Russians had nothing but good feelings toward Japan. The Diana was thereupon allowed to come to the port of Hakodate, where Golownin and his men were permitted to rejoin her.

ENGLISH ATTEMPTS TO TRADE WITH JAPAN

THE attempt of the English, in the reign of Charles II., to renew friendly relations with Japan, was not repeated. For more than a hundred years the Japanese were left undisturbed so far as England was concerned. At the end of the last century and the beginning of this, private merchants occasionally sent a ship to trade or barter, but, although these vessels were invariably supplied with whatever was needed, free of charge, communication with the shore was rendered impossible. The impressions left by such English vessels as succeeded in getting into Nagasaki harbor were not favorable to them.

In October, 1808, the British frigate Phaëton, Captain Pellew, had been commissioned to cruise off the coast of Japan, to capture the annual Dutch traders. For Holland had been annexed to France, and was therefore at war with England. For a month or more, Captain Pellew had been sailing over these seas without seeing a sign of any Dutch vessels. Thinking that they might be in the harbor of Nagasaki, he decided to look for himself. Flying Dutch colors, he approached that harbor, and as the usual Dutch vessel was expected at that time, she was permitted to anchor, and the general agent of the Dutch, suspecting nothing, sent two of his clerks to the frigate. They did not return, and this excited suspicion.

The Japanese governor decided at once to prepare for strong measures, but he found, to his dismay, that nearly all the soldiers of a strong fort in the harbor were absent without leave, and that the commandant was not to be found. A few hours later, the general agent received a brief note from one of the missing clerks, stating: "This ship has come from India. The captain's name is Pellew; he asks for water and provisions."

The general agent was afraid to comply without the consent of the governor. At midnight he was visited by the governor's chief secretary, who told him that he had orders to rescue the two Hollanders.

"How do you propose doing it?" asked the agent.

"Your countrymen have been seized by treachery," replied the secretary; "I shall therefore go alone, obtain admission on board by every demonstration of friendship, seek an interview with the captain, and on his refusal to deliver his prisoners, stab him first, and then myself."

It was with difficulty that this officer was persuaded to abandon his desperate plan, and it was finally decided to detain the frigate until all the boats, junks, and troops of the neighboring territories could be collected, and then to attack. The night was spent in warlike preparations, which, says the agent, who has written several works on Japan, "gave evidence that the country had been at peace for a very long time." The next afternoon, one of the missing Hollanders was put ashore. He brought a note stating: "I have ordered my own boat to set the bearer on shore, to procure me water and provisions; if he does not return with them before evening, I will sail in early to-morrow, and burn the Japanese and Chinese vessels in the harbor."

The Japanese official at first would not allow the clerk to return to the ship, but finally consented, upon the agent's reminding him that it was the only way to recover the other man. He, therefore, went on board with the provisions, and shortly afterwards the two clerks were set at liberty.

The governor now consulted with the agent concerning the execution of the law which obliged him to detain, till the decision of the head government was known, any foreign vessel which came too near, or committed any violent or illegal act on the coast. The agent told him plainly that he did not think the Japanese strong enough to detain the frigate; but he advised him to try to occupy the captain's attention until a number of native ships, loaded with stones, could be sunk in the narrow passage through which the frigate must proceed to sea. The Japanese harbor master thought that this could be done, and received orders to make the necessary preparations. Another supply of fresh water was promised to the frigate to detain her while a favorable wind was blowing.

The next morning the daimio of Omura arrived at the head of his samurai, and proposed to the governor to burn the frigate by attacking her with three hundred boats, filled with straw and reeds; he himself offered to lead the attack. But while they were consulting, the frigate weighed anchor, and sailed out of the harbor.

Were the governor and the officials of Nagasaki in any way responsible for this incident, or could they be blamed at all for the course they had taken? According to our ideas they were absolutely innocent, but the Japanese law said otherwise. The rules and laws of the government had been broken, and those who had not prevented or punished this, must die. Within half an hour after the frigate's departure, the governor had redeemed himself from a severer fate by committing hara-kiri. The officers of the fortress, who had been guilty of neglect of duty, followed his example. These men were of the clan of Hizen, and their daimio, who was actually residing in Yedo at the time, was punished with one hundred days' imprisonment for the negligence of his samurai. Such was the law, and sufferers as well as others consented and approved.

The next attempt by the English was made in 1813. Great Britain had seized the Dutch East Indies, and Sir Stamford Raffles had been appointed governor general of Java. He decided to capture the profitable Japanese trade for England, and did not expect any difficulties, because the Dutch at Nagasaki were ignorant of the changes that had occurred during the past years. The seas were controlled by English vessels, and several years had passed without the appearance of the usual Dutch trader, hence the general agent was very much pleased when two vessels, flying the Dutch flag, and showing the private signal, entered the harbor.

As soon as they had anchored, a letter was sent ashore, announcing the arrival of a former general agent, who had come to replace the agent in charge. The latter, without any suspicion, sent an officer and a clerk on board. The clerk returned and reported that he could not quite understand what was going on, but that he feared everything was not right. He had, to be sure, recognized the former general agent, and also the Dutch captain of the ship, but the crew spoke English, and the new general agent had refused to deliver his credentials, except to the agent in person. That gentleman thought naturally that the ship might be an American vessel engaged by the Dutch, as had been the case before, and decided upon going aboard.

There the former general agent handed him a letter, which, however, he declined to open until he was in his office. Both gentlemen thereupon went ashore to the office, and when the letter was opened, the bewildered agent, who for four years had heard nothing of the world beyond Nagasaki, read about the changes that had taken place. The letter informed him that the former general agent had been appointed his successor with the title of Commissary in Japan, and was signed "Raffles, Lieutenant Governor of Java, and its dependencies."

"Raffles! Who is Raffles?" asked the puzzled agent.

His former friend now explained that Java had been captured by the English; that Holland no longer existed as an independent nation, but had become a part of the French empire, and that he, the former general agent, and an Englishman, Dr. Ainslie, had been appointed by the British government as commissioners in Japan.

The Dutch agent did not hesitate as soon as he was in possession of these facts. He refused absolutely to obey the orders conveyed in the letter, stating that they came from a colony in possession of the enemy; that Japan was in no way a dependency of Java, nor was she at all affected by any capitulation into which the Dutch in Java might have entered with the English.

The attempt was foolish in the extreme. The ships were unarmed, and if the agent had informed the governor, or suffered the secret to leak out, short shrift would have been given to their English crews. For the affair of the Phaeton was still fresh in the memory of the Japanese, and they were anxious to obtain revenge. The agent hated the English, who had caused such severe losses to his countrymen; but the old general agent was his friend and patron, and the Dutch agent agreed to keep his own counsel upon certain conditions benefiting his countrymen. These were agreed to. The cargoes of the two vessels were delivered in the usual manner; the vessels were loaded with copper, and the English sailed away without having aroused the suspicions of the Japanese.

The following year Lieutenant Governor Raffles made another attempt to wield influence over Japan, but it failed completely. In 1818, Captain Gordon of the British navy sailed up Yedo Bay and made a formal request to be allowed to return with a cargo, for the purpose of trading. This request was politely but firmly refused. The captain was treated with the greatest kindness and good will, provisions were offered him, and anything of which he might be in need; but he was given to understand that only two nations, the Dutch and the Chinese, were permitted to trade with Japan, and only at Nagasaki.

In the year 1831, a Japanese junk, blown off the coast into the Pacific Ocean, after drifting about for a long time, went ashore near the mouth of the Columbia River. The castaways were kindly treated, and in 1835 were taken to Macao, a Portuguese settlement in China, where they were cared for by the American and English residents. It was decided to seize this opportunity to open intercourse with Japan. An American merchantman, the Morrison, well equipped for the purpose, was engaged, and her arms and ammunition were left behind in token of her peaceable intentions.

It was thought by the promoters of this enterprise that the return of shipwrecked fellow-countrymen would be appreciated. They did not know of the cruel Japanese law: "All Japanese who return from abroad, shall be put to death." With a medical missionary on board, the Morrison left Macao, and arrived without accident in Yedo Bay. After she had anchored, she was visited by officers from the shore, who carefully examined into her strength. When they discovered that she was wholly unarmed, they showed the greatest insolence and contempt, and the following morning opened fire upon her. She was compelled to weigh anchor in a hurry, and, leaving this bay, sailed westward, anchoring off Kagoshima (kah-goh'-shee-mah), in the island of Kiushiu.

Here one of the passengers, Mr. C. W. King, a New York merchant, decided to open negotiations with the emperor (regent). He prepared a paper in which he said:—

"The American vessels sail faster than those of other nations. If permitted to have intercourse with Japan, they will always communicate the latest intelligence. . . . Our countrymen have not yet visited your honorable country, but only know that, in old times, the merchants of all nations were admitted to your harbors. Afterwards, having transgressed the law, they were restricted or expelled. Now we, coming for the first time, and not having done wrong, request permission to carry on a friendly intercourse on the ancient footing."

The natives of Kiushiu appeared well disposed and even friendly; but, after some time, striped canvas cloths were being stretched along the shore. The rescued Japanese told their American friends that this meant mischief; that cannon were being placed, and that firing would soon commence. The anchor was weighed, and when the vessel sailed, a battery opened upon her. The plan was therefore abandoned, and, the Morrison returned to Macao.

In 1845 Nagasaki was visited, first by the British frigate Samarang, Captain Sir Edward Belcher, and later by Admiral Cecille (say-seel) in the French ship Cléopâtre (clay-oh-pahtr). Both were politely received, but secured no advantage beyond a liberal supply of provisions and water. Indeed, they were given to understand that these visits were not welcome; that Japan asked no favors, and desired none. But when a Japanese, in his private capacity, expressed an opinion, a thing not to be thought of unless he was sure to be out of earshot of any of his countrymen, he would declare that the people were in favor of opening their country to foreigners. It was indeed the government that insisted upon maintaining the seclusion as begun by Iyeyasu, and strengthened and made more burdensome by his successors. The regents, or those who ruled in their names, were afraid that intercourse with foreigners would cause their downfall,—and they were right, as we shall soon see.

THE UNITED STATES SEEKS TRADE WITH JAPAN

NEW BEDFORD, Massachusetts, had begun to send whaling vessels into the Pacific Ocean, and Japan was so conveniently situated to obtain provisions after the long passage over the Atlantic and Pacific, that the President decided to make an effort to enter into a treaty of friendship with that government. Accordingly President James K. Polk commissioned Commodore Biddle to go to Yedo with two ships, the Columbus, a line-of-battle ship, and the Vincennes, a sloop of war, to deliver a letter to His Imperial Majesty of Japan. This letter was in substance as follows:—

"I send you, by this letter, an envoy of my own appointment, an officer of high rank in his country, who is no missionary of religion. He goes by my command to bear to you my greeting and good wishes, and to promote friendship and commerce between the two countries.

"You know that the United States of America now extend from sea to sea; that the great countries of Oregon and California are parts of the United States; and that from these countries, which are rich in gold and silver and precious stones, our steamers can reach the shores of your happy land in less than twenty days.

"Many of our ships will now pass every year, and some, perhaps, every week, between California and China; these ships must pass along the coasts of your empire; storms and winds may cause them to be wrecked on your shores, and we ask and expect from your friendship and your greatness, kindness for our men and protection for our property. We wish that our people may be permitted to trade with your people; but we shall not authorize them to break any law of your empire.

"Our object is friendly commercial intercourse, and nothing more. You may have productions which we should be glad to buy, and we have productions which might suit your people.

"Your empire contains a great abundance of coal; this is an article which our steamers, in going from California to China, must use. They would be glad that a harbor in your empire should be appointed to which coal might be brought, and where they might always be able to purchase it.

"In many other respects commerce between your empire and our country would be useful to both. Let us consider well what new interests may arise from these recent events, which have brought our two countries so near together, and what purpose of friendly amity and intercourse this ought to inspire in the hearts of those who govern both countries."

The commodore arrived at the entrance of Yedo Bay in July, 1846. Before his vessels had fairly anchored, they were surrounded by about four hundred guard boats, which, however, showed no sign of hostility, since the men, of whom each boat contained from five to twenty, were mostly unarmed. An inferior officer climbed up the side of the Vincennes, and proceeded to place a stick with some Chinese symbol on it, at the bow, and a similar one at the stern. The captain construed this act to mean taking possession of his ship and therefore at once ordered the sticks removed, to which the Japanese offered no objection.

The letter was now given to one of the officers, and an interpreter came aboard who spoke Dutch fluently. There was no attempt to communicate with the shore, but the officials who came on board gave no evidence of dislike for foreigners. Like all Japanese of the samurai class, they were studiously polite, and exceedingly anxious to obtain information. On the seventh day an answer came from Yedo. It was brief, but to the point: "No trade can be allowed with any foreign nation, except Holland." What could Commodore Biddle do? He had no instructions to employ force, and therefore was compelled to return without having accomplished anything.

But the government in Washington did not despair. A Japanese junk, on the way from Yedo to Osaka, was caught in a storm and blown out into the Pacific Ocean. The poor sailors did not know where they were, and for three weeks drifted at the mercy of wind and waves. At last one of those strange vessels, such as they had sometimes seen at Nagasaki, was sighted, and they made signals of distress. The vessel hove to; the Japanese launched their boat, rowed to the ship, and were taken on board, where they were very kindly treated. This ship was bound for San Francisco, and when she arrived, the United States officers were told of the passengers taken up in mid-ocean. They communicated with the government in Washington, and received orders to take care of the Japanese until they could be sent back to their country.

Among these sailors was a fourteen-year-old boy. He learned very quickly to speak English, and became a great pet of the naval officers at Mare Island, California. At last, when he knew our language, he found a friend in a gentleman of San Francisco, who had him educated, and took him to Baltimore and Washington. As the boy grew up, he attended Sunday school and became a Christian, and when he was old enough, he took out his naturalization papers; that is, he declared that thereafter he would obey the laws of the United States, and was made an American citizen. He afterwards returned to Japan, where he was very useful as an interpreter, and could explain American institutions and laws to the officers.

In 1849 Commodore Geisinger sent the Preble, under Commander Glynn, to Japan to demand the release of some American seamen who had been cast ashore from the wreck of the whaler Lagoda. When the Preble approached Japan, she was warned to return, by a great display of batteries "in petticoats," as the sailors called them, because lines of striped canvas cloth, stretched one behind the other, were used to deaden the shot, as well as to conceal the gunners. When the Preble paid no attention to these warlike demonstrations, but quietly continued on her course, a paper, attached to the end of a long bamboo stick, and containing some directions in English, was offered to the captain, who, however, declined to accept it, but sailed on.

Then an interpreter came on board, and ordered the captain to anchor at a certain spot. But the captain showed him a chart, and pointed out the spot where he had decided to stop. Now some officers of inferior rank came on board to ask about the captain's business, but he refused to receive them. At last officers of a high rank came on board, and they were informed of the purpose of his visit. They said that they wanted time to be able to consult with the emperor (regent). But the commander of the Preble answered that he would give them just so many days, and no more. The Japanese understood the threat, and in a very short time the American sailors were sent aboard. The Japanese then offered to supply the ship with provisions and water, but as they refused payment, the American captain very properly declined to accept their offer.

HOW PERRY SECURED A TREATY

WHEN Commander James Glynn returned to Washington in 1851, after his visit to Nagasaki in the Preble, he began to try to interest the President to make another effort to open Japan, and offered his services. But when the matter was taken into consideration, it became clear that a few ships would not be able to accomplish anything peaceably, and that, to insure success, it was necessary to send an imposing fleet. When, finally, it was decided that the United States should act, Commodore Aulick was selected to go to the capital of the Tycoon, and to present a letter from the President to "the emperor of Japan."

Commodore Aulick sailed from Norfolk, Virginia, June 1851, in the Susquehanna, and after stopping at the capital of Brazil, continued his voyage to China. Soon after he had arrived at Hong Kong, he received orders to return home, and Commodore Matthew G. Perry, brother of the hero who upheld the honor of the American flag on Lake Erie, was appointed to replace him.

There had been, before this, some talk about Perry's undertaking this mission, and he had spent considerable time in reading all the books on Japan he could find. From what he had gleaned of the Japanese character, Perry felt confident that with a strong force under his command, he could awe the Japanese into making concessions, whereas a small fleet would probably be treated with contempt. He was promised twelve vessels with which to proceed to Yedo Bay, and thereupon began to make preparations.

First he arranged to have ships laden with coal, dispatched to the Cape of Good Hope and Mauritius (maw-rish'-i-us), that his steamers might obtain there a fresh supply of fuel. Next he began to collect specimens of American industries and inventions. A firm in Philadelphia furnished a small locomotive, and rails to be laid down in Japan. He also took with him a telegraph and other new inventions with which you are familiar enough, but which could not fail to impress a people so fond of examining and appropriating anything new and useful. Finally the letter was prepared. You may be sure that it was no ordinary letter, but an imposing state paper. It was locked in a gold box that cost a thousand dollars, and this was securely hidden in a rosewood casket with golden hinges.

The commodore waited for a long time for the ships that had been promised him, but at last he grew tired of delays, and on November 24, 1852, sailed from Norfolk in the Mississippi. After stopping at several places on her journey, the Mississippi anchored at Hong Kong, April 6, 1853, and shortly afterwards, accompanied by the Plymouth, Saratoga, and Supply, left for Shanghai, arriving May 4, Perry now went on board the Susquehanna, and after visiting the Loo Choo and other islands, sailed for Yedo Bay on July 2, 1853. Of the twelve vessels promised to him, only six had put in an appearance, and as he sent back the Supply and the Caprice, the "imposing force" consisted of only four ships, the Mississippi, Susquehanna, Plymouth, and Saratoga, of which two were sailing vessels. It was, therefore, not the force displayed by the government of the United States, which impressed the regent's officers; but, as we shall see, the calm and proud bearing of the commodore.

At last the goal of the expedition, Yedo Bay, was reached, and in the afternoon of July 8, the vessels anchored. The order was given: "No one allowed to go ashore, no person from the shore to be allowed on board," and it was not long before the wisdom of this order became apparent. The foreign captains who had up to this time visited Yedo Bay had taken orders from the first officer showing the two swords of the samurai, and the Yedo government had begun to look with contempt upon foreigners who would submissively obey the orders of one of its lower officials. But on this occasion no respect was paid to any individual before his rank was known. Even the vice governor was refused admittance! And not until he stated, without regard to truth, that the laws of Japan forbade the governor from going aboard a foreign ship, was he permitted to put his foot on deck.

He wanted to see the commander at once! Ah, yes, but the commander was too great a person to be seen by so insignificant a man as Mr. Vice Governor. "Tell him, then, to go back to Nagasaki!" "Oh! but the Commander is too great a man to be told such a thing. Mr. Vice Governor could be sure that this Great Man would not listen to such talk. And, by the bye, Mr. Vice Governor, you had better send those guard boats away from these ships, or the Great Man might get angry, and then . . ." The gravity of the speaker impressed the native visitor. This line of conduct he could understand. It was in this manner that a powerful Japanese officer would have acted. His report brought the governor himself the next day in all the pomp of lacquered helmet, two swords, silks, etc., despite the vice governor's colored statement of the day before.

Down on their knees, with heads bent to touch the bottom of their boats, were the attendants of this mighty person, as he ascended the gangway of the "fire ship." But even he was not allowed a personal interview with the mysterious commander. "Go back to Nagasaki? He had not come for that purpose. He had a letter to the emperor in Yedo, and to Yedo he would go." "Would he wait four days so that the emperor could be appealed to, and an answer be received?" "No, he would consent to wait three days, but not a moment longer; and in the meanwhile his boats would do some surveying." "No, that can't be done. No surveying under any circumstances!" "Ah, but the Great Man has ordered it, and who will oppose him?"

The Japanese governor went ashore, convinced that these were the most intractable foreigners he had ever met, and that this mysterious Great Man must be very great indeed, to have things all his own way!

The next day there was another visit. But the governor was told that no strangers would be allowed on board, not even the emperor himself. It was Sunday, and Commodore Perry was not the man to break the Sabbath for slight causes. The blunt statement about the regent—for we know now that the regent in Yedo had no right to the title of emperor—increased the respect of the Japanese; and it was only in a half-hearted way, and without any hope that they would be able to frighten the Great Man, that they began to throw up earthworks, and to collect an army of knights, clothed in rusty armor of the Middle Ages.

It was unwelcome news, brought to the Yedo government, when runners arrived with a detailed account of the four vessels and the mysterious person in command. It was evident that something must be done at once. But the foreigners with whom the "descendants of the gods" had dealt so far, had been satisfied to confer with petty officers, and custom could not be discarded at once. At last it was decided to send two squires to take charge of the letter to the regent.

And so the governor received orders to communicate to the Great Man that the "emperor" would commission two princes to receive the letter on shore. You see that Perry had well understood the Japanese. They thought these two squires were good enough princes to deal with barbarians. But Perry was not to be outdone. He did not know that these were sham princes, but he gave the governor to understand that it was not meet for an officer of his sublime rank to go so far from the anchorage in a boat, and so he moved his steamers within convenient range of the place appointed. And now the time came when oriental pomp was to be rivaled by occidental gold lace.

Through the three hundred sailors and marines, drawn up as on parade, marched the commodore with his staff. And here again he had taken the only means to awe his unwilling hosts. They gazed upon the two powerful sailors carrying the Stars and Stripes, upon the two boys bearing that mysterious red casket, and upon the two stalwart negroes, acting as guard. The Americans entered the temporary building erected for the purpose, and after the casket was opened and the letter displayed, it was handed to one of the sham princes, who was introduced as "The First Councilor of the Empire." Then a formal reply was delivered by the interpreter, to this effect: "We have received the letter of the President of the United States of North America. We have let you know that we don't care about having foreigners here, and if you want anything from us you must go to Nagasaki. Your mysterious Great Man made us believe that he would be insulted if we did not receive the letter at this place. Very well, we have done so. The answer we will give you later, and now you may go home."

"All right," said Commodore Perry, cheerfully. "And when shall I call for an answer? Don't be too anxious to see me soon! Shall we say April or May next year?" And he returned on board, leaving the "princes" convinced that they had not yet seen the last of him.

While Perry was in Hong Kong, where his ships were being repaired, he received an official communication through the Dutch at Deshima that the "emperor" was dead, and that it would be well if he postponed his promised call. But the commodore had obtained such strong evidence that the Japanese did not always stick to the truth, and could even invent facts on occasion, that he did not believe the report, but, suspecting some trick, rather hurried his preparations.

And yet, the news received was correct, except that it was not the emperor but the regent who was dead. This, however, did not materially alter the circumstances. All that the Japanese hoped for was delay; but Perry spoiled their plans by his prompt action.

In January, 1854, the fleet, consisting of the Macedonian, Vandalia, Lexington, Southampton, Saratoga, and Supply, with the steamers Susquehanna, Mississippi, and Powhatan, once more left for Japan. The commodore again stopped at the Loo Choo Islands, so as to give the sailing vessels a good start, and on Monday, the 13th of February, the fleet moved up Yedo Bay, the steamers towing the sailing vessels, until they came within about seven miles from where Yokohama now stands. This was only about twenty-five miles from Yedo, and so unpleasantly close that the regent's government decided: "Well, if these persistent people must have a treaty, we cannot help ourselves; only we must grant as little as possible." And now the play of the mysterious Great Man was to be acted once more.

"Where would the Great Man prefer the negotiations to take place?" they asked, mentioning two places at a great distance from the capital. The reply, after consulting with the invisible commodore, was:—

"Never mind about those places. The spot opposite us will do as well as any other."

This answer did not suit. The Japanese tried flattery, coaxing, little presents, all to no avail. Finally they were told that the Great Man would very much like to have matters arranged by February 21; that, in fact, he would take no refusal. And so the Japanese sighed: "Well, it can't be helped! But where will you have it?" "Oh!" replied the commodore, still invisible, "I think that Yedo would be the best place." But that would not do at all. Perry sent some of his men ashore at Uraga (oo-rah-gah) to confer about a meeting place and waited until February 24; then he advanced another eight miles, anchoring a little beyond Yokohama. Afraid that he would go still nearer to the capital, the government yielded, and the negotiations were held at Yokohama, which is only a short distance from Yedo.

This time the commodore landed with five hundred well-armed men, and, after long and tedious discussions, a treaty was made on March 31, 1854. By the terms of the treaty American ships could enter the harbors of Hakodate in Hokkaido, and Shimoda (shee-moh-dah) in Hondo, for coal, water, and provisions, and their sailors would be kindly treated. There was also an article promising trading facilities as well as several other privileges. And now came the exchange of presents. Perry presented the telegraph, with one mile of wire, the little locomotive and car, rifles, guns, clocks, sewing machines, maps, charts, etc., and the Japanese gave lacquer, bronze, porcelain, ivory, silk, all of which you may see in the Smithsonian Institute, at Washington. Perry then returned home, having succeeded where so many had failed.

JAPAN IN PERRY'S TIME

WE must now look at Japan as it was when Commodore Perry was on his way to tell its government: "You can no longer refuse the hand of friendship we are holding out to you. It is absurd to suppose that, because of a mere whim, our ships will avoid your shores. We do not propose to take any advantage of you; but we ask you to sell us what we need, and you can, if you wish, buy from us what you may need. At any rate, we do not purpose to stay away from your country simply because you would like us to." Perry, as we have seen, was the right man to carry this message.

For two hundred and fifty years the descendants of Iyeyasu had ruled over Japan. During all this time there had been peace at home and abroad, owing to the strict laws, the perfect system of spying, and the exclusion of foreigners. The people worked hard and made a living; but as they could not sell in the markets abroad, they received very small pay. There was, however, no poverty, that is, suffering from want; nor was there any great wealth. If the people had enough rice, vegetables, fish, and clothing to cover themselves, what more did they require? Thus the great masses of the people were contented and happy,—but how about the samurai?

For some two hundred and fifty years their swords had been sheathed. They had busied themselves with the affairs of their clans; but that did not occupy all their time. To be sure, they could pay and receive calls from their friends, and show their intimate knowledge of the ceremonies inseparable from a tea party. They knew exactly the deference due to a person, and the number of compliments he was entitled to. But even the acquisition of this knowledge left them considerable leisure, and they spent it in reading.

The samurai from the time of Nobunaga, who, as we have seen, made war upon the ambitious monks, held Buddhism in contempt. They turned to the study of the pure Shinto religion, which regards the Tennô as divine and worships the ancestors as gods. But when they began to study the history of their country, when they understood that this regent in Yedo, before whom they were compelled to bow, was only a usurper, and that the Tennô, and the Tennô only, was the lawful ruler of Japan, they looked around for means to deny the authority of the regent.

A very large number of the samurai read with absorbing attention the history of Japan, completed under the second daimio of Mito, who was a descendant of Iyeyasu; and another history written by Rai Sanyo (ri-sahn-yoh), wherein it was shown that the loyalty of the samurai was due to the Tennô, was also extensively studied. The reading of these books made them all the more impatient of the Tokugawa rule.

"Are we less brave and less stout than our fathers?" they would ask. "Why must our swords remain sheathed? Who is responsible for these long years of contemptible peace? Why can we not subdue Korea, which by law of conquest belongs to Japan?" There was deep dissatisfaction among the samurai, and while they were not able to express all they felt, of one thing they were very sure, —that they no longer wanted the descendants of Iyeyasu to rule over them.

The great daimio of the south, those of Satsuma, Choshiu (choh-shoo), and Tosa, were especially hostile to the regent. The trade with Holland, which was very profitable, was for the benefit of the Yedo government. Through the Hollanders, the regent could know what was passing abroad; he could order the latest guns and cannon, and thereby acquire the means to keep the daimio in submission. All these daimio encouraged, therefore, the reading of these books, and urged their men to arouse the Yamato Damashii (yah-mah-toh dah-mah-shee-ee)—that is, the Spirit of Old Japan—among the people.

But the regent in Yedo could afford to laugh at all this discontent so long as the daimio remained divided among themselves. Even if the most powerful among them should dare deny his authority, eighty thousand of his own samurai were prepared to punish a rebel. And besides, the loyal daimio, descendants of Iyeyasu or of his generals, were ready to take up arms in his defense. There was only the fear that the disaffected daimio might unite, that they might march upon Kyoto and obtain the sacred person of the emperor,—then, and then only, would there be an end to the Tokugawa rule.

Kyoto was the key to the situation. But there was a strong garrison composed of the samurai of the most loyal clan, guarding the palace, and the admittance to Kyoto was strictly prohibited to any of the southern daimio. So long as the emperor remained in the power of the Tokugawa, all was well. The court nobles,—who and what were they? Paupers, glad enough to be fed from the crumbs of the regent's bounty.

But how about the regent himself? Was he the same able, self-reliant man that Iyeyasu, the founder of the house, had been? No. The Tokugawa had gone the way of all the rulers of Japan. Seven regents had succeeded from the direct line, and then successors had been adopted. For a long time the descendants of Iyeyasu had been shadow regents,—puppets in the hands of ambitious prime ministers, who trusted to their spies to maintain their power.

Dissatisfaction existed everywhere. But while the great majority of samurai would have been well pleased to see the authority restored to the emperor, the ablest among them desired to be his personal advisers; in other words, they wished for themselves the power held by the Tokugawa. Satsuma thought that it would be better for Japan if he should be regent, the other great daimio had probably the same idea regarding themselves, and their kerai (kay-ri), or councilors, thought how much better it would be if they could direct the affairs. But neither daimio nor samurai had any idea of personal gain; they honestly believed they were right. And they would have been pleased to accept this power without any salary, except just enough to secure the absolute necessities of life for themselves and their families.

It was sure to go hard with the government of Yedo when the opportunity for action came. Hundreds of samurai were ready to sever the connection with their clan and turn rônin, if they could thereby assist in over-turning the Tokugawa. What cared they if hara-kiri must inevitably follow? They were prepared for it. Were not the graves of the forty-seven free lances kept green in the memory of the people, and would not they also be celebrated in song and story? What greater desire could a true samurai have than to die in the service of his clan and his lord?

Many of the samurai were not so ignorant as they seemed. Some of them had studied Dutch; and although all the books on board a Dutch vessel arriving at Nagasaki were supposed to be stored in chests and kept under lock and key in possession of the regent's officers, to be returned only when the ship was ready to sail, this did not prevent the inquisitive and studious Japanese from obtaining possession of some of them. And these barbarian vessels that were coming so repeatedly, notwithstanding the regent's prohibition, would they insist upon breaking the laws of Japan? Was it not true that the king of Holland had sent a letter, advising the regent to enter into a treaty with these hairy (bearded) strangers? And was it not true also that these same barbarians had dared invade the soil of China, and compelled that great empire to grant their demands? Would they also dare come with an armed force to sacred Japan, the country of the gods, and profane the land destined for the Japanese? Or would the Tokugawa at Yedo repeat the disgrace inflicted upon Japan by the cowardly Ashikaga? These were the questions that agitated the samurai, those four hundred thousand men who had been and were then at once the head and the arms of the country, who ruled as well as defended it.

They were thinking and watching. They felt instinctively that the time for action was drawing nigh; and all of them were sure that the samurai of Japan would be able, when the time came, to give a lesson to the barbarians. They wished to have their coast defenses strengthened, and requested the Yedo government to attend to this. No notice was taken of this request. The councilors of the regent, troubled about affairs at home, hoped and trusted that foreign powers would continue to respect their absolute refusal to enter into intercourse with them.

Every foreign vessel entering the Japanese waters was received by officers, who were naturally Tokugawa men; that is, men belonging to the clan of the regent. And while many of them were in favor of more liberal measures, they were loyal to those who stood at the head of their clan, and were prepared to carry out their orders. Captains of such foreign vessels could not judge, therefore, of the actual feeling prevailing among the Japanese, since these men represented only the Tokugawa clan.

When, at last, compulsion made the regent grant the demands of the self-invited guests, the Tokugawa samurai were fully satisfied. But not so those of other clans. They could not, and did not, deny that since a Tokugawa regent had taken it upon himself to exclude foreigners, another regent of the same house could rescind or abolish this law by his own authority. What they did object to was the manner in which permission to trade with and to reside in Japan had been obtained: that a regent of Japan should have submitted to demands from foreigners without striking a blow! Had he granted the requests of petitioners, and had he opened such ports as would have given to every daimio the opportunity to profit by this intercourse, the Tokugawa regents might have secured another lease of government. But the government of Yedo thought that they would be able to isolate these newcomers as they had the Dutch, and so opened only such ports as belonged to the Tokugawa. This caused the hatred, both against the Yedo government and the foreigners, and the many murders of innocent men by self-appointed avengers.

JAPAN OPENED

THE first treaty with Japan was signed. It did not grant many privileges, but our government saw that an opening had been effected, and seized the opportunity to improve it.

In those days hundreds of American ships were trading on the coast of China, and many of our merchants went there themselves, so that they obtained considerable experience in dealing with oriental people. One of these merchants, Townsend Harris, of the state of New York, was appointed the first United States consul in Japan.

When the British and Russians saw that the United States had succeeded in making a treaty, they wanted to obtain the same privileges. England sent an embassy under Lord Elgin, and now, what could the government at Yedo do? The foreigners were not wanted; but the visitors would take no refusal, and Japan was not in condition to defend itself. Should it call the samurai to arms? You may be sure that all would have responded eagerly, but the regent's ministers knew that the utmost courage was no match for modern cannon, and that soldiers with armor and bow and arrow could not defeat the forces that would be sent against them. No, the foreigners must be allowed to come; that was inevitable. But the government could try to keep these barbarians apart from the Japanese, and then if the trade did not prove profitable, they would, perhaps, go away of their own accord.

But these foreigners, now they had once entered, were not satisfied to remain cooped up. They did not obey the officers appointed to watch them, but would claim that they had rights which they would uphold, even if the government did not wish them to do so.

And then there was trouble at home. The regent was dead, and had left no son. The daimio of Mito, a descendant of Iyeyasu, wanted one of his sons appointed; but that did not suit the daimio of Hikone (hee-koh'-nay), who was prime minister, and a very able but unscrupulous man. If Mito's son were appointed, his father would be the real regent, and Ii Naosuke (ee-ee-nah-oh-skay), the Lord of Hikone, wished to retain his power. Ii gained the day, and his candidate, Iyemochi (ee-yay-moh-chee), succeeded as regent.

But now the foreigners were no longer satisfied with the port of Shimoda. There had been a tidal wave, and the Diana, a Russian man-of-war, had been wrecked in Shimoda, so that port was considered unsafe. At last the regent's government was compelled to allow them to come and live in Kanagawa (kah-nah-gah-wah).

And what do you think the Japanese samurai thought of all this? They had no idea at all of the strength and power of these foreigners. All they did know was that Japan, the land of the gods, had been invaded by them, and that they had forced the Tokugawa regents to give them a part of the sacred soil of their country. It is true that there were only a few of these barbarians now, but in the eyes of the Japanese theirs was such a desirable country that they feared these uninvited guests would be only the forerunners of the host that was to follow. And these Tokugawa had admitted them! They had submitted to the demands of the Tojin (toh-jin), that is, foreign imps, under threats! And thus a vague dread changed into hatred, and, "Down with the Tokugawa! Expel the barbarian!" became the rallying cry of Japan's warriors.

The foreign ministers knew nothing of the excitement caused by their admittance into Japan. In the treaty the regent had taken the title of Dai Kun (ty-coon), which means Great Prince, and although they had heard of a Mikado (Tennô), they were satisfied with the treaty made by the regent. Not so, however, the samurai. They knew now that the regent was only a servant of the Tennô, and that he had no authority whatever to give an inch of Japan's soil to these strangers. Yet he had done so. And now the daimio of Mito, his kinsman, remonstrated with him, and stated very plainly that all these acts were unlawful, because they had not been sanctioned by the Tennô.

And how was it in Kyoto? There the governor of the Yedo government kept a strict guard. Yet several great court nobles, or kuge (koo-gay), were watching with anxious eyes for the result of this new disturbance. I must tell you the names of two of these kuge, Sanjo and Iwakura (ee-wah-koo-rah), for they took a leading part in the revolution now so near at hand. These kuge, though poor, and supported, with the emperor's household, out of the scant allowance paid by the wealthy regents, were, in the eyes of the Japanese, superior in rank to the most powerful daimio, and even to the regent himself. Another man who was to take a prominent part in the making of New Japan, —a man closely related to the Tennô himself, whose title of Miya (mee-yah), or Temple, showed the high rank he held in the structure of which the Heaven Child was the cornerstone,—Prince Arisugawa (ah-ree-soo-gah-wah), was there to prompt the emperor to such action as his advisers might decide upon. It was evident that the influence of the Tokugawa was waning. And the kuge resolved to watch the course of events, and in the meanwhile to enter into communication with the daimio of the southern clans; for if the Tokugawa were to be overthrown, it must be done by them.

But a feud existed between the two wealthiest and most warlike of these clans, Satsuma and Choshiu, a feud carefully nursed by the government in Yedo. In both clans, however, there were, among the samurai, able men of great power and influence. Okubo (oh-koo-boh) and Saigo Takamori (si-goh tah-kah-moh-ree), and Kido (kee-do),—the first two Satsuma men, the last belonging to the Choshiu clan—saw that a union was necessary to overcome the strong power of the Tokugawa, and that there was only one authority in Japan that could bring the clans together, and that was the Tennô in Kyoto. They proceeded to that city, and placed themselves in communication with the kuge Sanjo and Iwakura, and it was decided to raise the cry of "Yamato Damashii (Spirit of Old Japan)! Expel the barbarians!"

Their main object was to save Japan from an invasion by foreigners, and then to punish the Tokugawa regents for the danger and disgrace they had brought upon their country. They did not and could not see any further. But after these purposes were accomplished, they could decide as to the future.

The foreigners now insisted that certain ports should be opened, where they could buy property, build houses, and trade. But in theory, at least, all the soil of Japan belonged to the Tennô, and how could the regent deed it away? Still the foreigners would take no refusal, and at last the government of Yedo promised to set apart some land in Kanagawa, where they could build their houses and live. It was, however, with great misgivings that this promise was made.

When the time came, Mr. Townsend Harris arrived and raised the American flag. But the merchants did not like Kanagawa, which is on a high bluff on the bay, where at ebb tide the water runs out and leaves extensive mud banks. They preferred the site of a little fishing village on the beach, Yokohama, and when the request for the change was made the Yedo government eagerly assented. For Kanagawa is on the main road by which all the southern daimio with their numerous escorts of samurai must pass on their annual journey to and from Yedo; and the regent's ministers foresaw trouble if the independent foreign merchants and the haughty samurai should meet.

The new treaty was signed in 1858, and the foreign settlement of Yokohama was begun in 1859. An American, Dr. Hall, who was with Mr. Townsend Harris, bought the first lot, and began building a handsome residence in our style of architecture.

Now foreign vessels began to arrive in Yokohama, for the Japanese people were glad to buy goods made abroad. But hundreds of samurai saw in the arrival of peaceful merchants the beginning of an invasion of their country, and thought that the best thing they could do was to cut down as many of these invaders as possible; and murders of foreigners in Yokohama became very frequent. The government dared not arrest the murderers, for very often they were prominent samurai of powerful clans. The foreign ministers demanded money for the men who were assassinated, or else that their murderers should be brought to justice, and the regent's government paid the money. A midshipman from the boat of a Russian man-of-war which had come to the beach for water, was almost cut in two by the sharp sword of a samurai. The government could not deliver up the murderer, so the Russian minister demanded that the northern half of the island of Saghalien (sah-gah-leen) should be given to Russia, and the Yedo government granted the demand. This looked very much as though the fears of the samurai that Japan might be divided among the foreigners were not groundless. The number of rônin increased, and it became dangerous for foreigners in Yokohama, even in broad daylight.

The foreign ministers had moved to Yedo, where each was given a temple to reside in, with a strong guard of Tokugawa samurai. But although the government did all it could to protect them, their residences were set on fire, and frequently they were attacked in the night. They were puzzled to know the reason of this hatred. The Japanese people—that is, the farmers, the merchants, and mechanics—were polite and civil, and showed no dislike for the foreigners. We know, now, however, that the samurai thought that their country was in danger, and they were willing to sacrifice their lives to drive the invaders away.

The ministers and the members of the legations were warned against going out. But one day Mr. Heusken, the secretary of the American minister, while on his way home, was cut down and killed. The Japanese government paid for this murder, but the assassin was never discovered. The other ministers decided to move to Yokohama, but Mr. Harris thought it best to remain in Yedo.

The government now committed a serious blunder. Thinking that it could appease the great clans by making some concessions, it abolished the law requiring the daimio to reside every other half year in Yedo. The samurai saw that the regent or his prime minister was afraid of them, and it only made them the bolder. The prime minister, Ii Naosuke, was the special object of their hatred, for he was considered the author of the treaties and the cause of the admission to Japan of the detested foreigners.

The daimio of Mito had not forgiven him for preventing his son from succeeding as regent, and he openly blamed the prime minister, while he praised the samurai who attacked defenseless foreigners. Ii punished him by banishing him to his seat in Mito. This was an insult to the clan which, according to the samurai code of honor, could only be wiped out in blood. Ii's life had been in constant danger, and he had taken precautions, but now his death was only a question of time.

On March 23, 1860, there was a heavy snowstorm in Yedo. Only those who were forced to leave their homes were hurrying through the deserted, snow-covered streets. After the prime minister had ordered his norimono (sedan chair) to proceed to the castle, his topknot became unfastened. This was such a sign of ill omen, that his attendants begged him to omit, or at least postpone, his daily visit. But Ii only laughed, and, as soon as his hair had been dressed, left his yashiki, with his escort. His samurai, to defend themselves against the inclement weather, had put on kimono (kee-moh-noh)—cotton gowns worn by men and women alike—and wore besides straw rain coats. As they were approaching the Sakura (sah-koo-rah) gate of the castle, the vanguard of the escort had an altercation with some people who seemed to be lounging there. The norimono halted, and Ii looked out to inquire into the cause of this stopping. Before the rear guard could run up, and throw off their rain coats to draw their swords, the norimono was surrounded by rônin, the prime minister's head was cut off, and the murderers escaped with their ghastly trophy. The head was taken to Mito, where it was placed upon a pike over the castle gate.

Among the clans who showed especial hostility to the admittance of foreigners was that of Choshiu in the south. Two young samurai of this clan, Ito (ee-to) and Inouye (ee-noo-yay), disregarding the risk of punishment by death if ever they should return to Japan, resolved to go to Europe and see for themselves if there was really any plan for the conquest of Japan. They obtained a passage to England, where they supported themselves in humble capacities, and mastered the English language. As soon as they were able to read and understand the newspapers, they discovered that nothing threatened the independence of their country, but they stood aghast when they fully comprehended how far Japan was behind the times. They returned to Japan at a critical time, when their services were valuable not only to their clan but also to their late hosts.

And here let me call attention to the all-absorbing love of country, so universal among the samurai. For their country's benefit these young men were willing to go among strangers, where they were treated with contempt as barbarians,—strangers, too, whose manners and customs were repugnant to them; and they were even content to serve them in a menial capacity, doing the humblest kind of work. For Ito, who was prime minister of Japan for many years, and who wrote the constitution, and Inouye, who was minister of state, ambassador to Korea, and held other prominent positions in the government, worked in England as house servants.

Choshiu's samurai were plotting in Kyoto, and Saigo Takamori, a very influential Satsuma samurai, whose sad story I shall tell you in another chapter, was helping them. But the plot leaked out, and the leading kuge were banished. Soon after this the Satsuma and Choshiu clans refused to obey any more orders from the regent, and when the Tokugawa sent an army to punish Choshiu, the government troops were badly defeated.

This emboldened these southern clans to begin open war upon the foreigners. If you look at the map of Japan, you will see that the southern part of Hondo is separated from the northern part of Kiushiu by the Straits of Shimonoseki (shee-moh-noh-say-kee). The government of Yedo had granted to foreigners the right to sail through these waters, but Choshiu, in whose territory Shimonoseki was situated, erected batteries, and when an American merchant ship, the Pembroke, was passing through the Straits, the Choshiu batteries opened fire upon her.

It happened that a sloop of war, the Wyoming, was in Yokohama harbor, where she had arrived after an unsuccessful search for the Alabama, the Confederate vessel that was doing so much harm to the merchantmen of the North. The American minister in Yedo now came to the conclusion that the regent's government was unable to control the southern daimio, and that, if these constant assaults were to cease, they must be stopped by the foreigners themselves; so he conferred with Captain David MacDougal of the Wyoming, who was quite willing to teach the Choshiu clan respect for the American flag.

He left for Shimonoseki and entered the Straits July 16, 1863. There were a steamer and a brig belonging to Choshiu, lying close in shore and under the batteries. The Choshiu samurai were glad enough to fight, but they were taken aback not a little when this single vessel, by skillful handling, in one hour and a half sunk their brig, blew up their steamer, and destroyed one of their batteries. They had also fired upon a French dispatch vessel, and a man-of-war of that nation destroyed another battery. But these defeats did not discourage the warriors of Choshiu. They needed another lesson before they would acknowledge that they were not so strong as these "foreign devils."

While this was going on in the south, the samurai of Choshiu, who had made Kyoto their headquarters, made an attempt to take the palace and to carry off the Tennô, because then they could issue orders in his name, and the regent in Yedo would be a rebel if he disobeyed their commands. But Satsuma and another clan rushed to the defense of the Tennô, because the Satsuma samurai did not want Choshiu to take the place of the Tokugawa, and at this time there were but a few individuals in Japan who had ever thought that the Heaven Child himself should engage in temporal affairs. The prevailing desire was to reclaim the government from the Tokugawa and to appoint a stronger man as barbarian-expelling regent. Many clans were ambitious to acquire this honor, but the most prominent were Satsuma, Choshiu, and Tosa. A battle was fought in the streets of Kyoto, where thirty thousand houses were destroyed by fire. Choshiu was defeated, and that clan was prohibited from ever reentering the capital.

The representative of the Satsuma clan was in Kyoto and proposed to escort to Yedo one of the kuge who was charged by the court with orders from the Tennô to the regent; commanding him to expel the barbarians. The prime minister had been informed of the purpose of this journey, and when Satsuma arrived in Yedo, refused to receive him. The old lord and his retainers were in no pleasant mood when they began their long return march.

They had gone about fourteen miles, with all the pomp of the Middle Ages, when they met a party of foreigners on horseback. They were three Englishmen and a lady. One of them, Mr. Richardson, was a merchant from Shanghai on his way to England for a vacation. They were going to visit a temple at Kawasaki (kah-wah-sah-kee) when they met Satsuma's escort. Japanese etiquette demanded that people on horseback should dismount while the procession of a daimio passed. It does not appear whether Mr. Richardson and his friends knew of this rule; but, even if they did, foreigners were not expected to conform to the rules of courtesy of the Japanese. It is said, however, that Mr. Richardson guided his horse through the procession, which, if true, was a foolhardy proceeding. Be that as it may, sharp swords flew out of their scabbards, and in a few minutes Mr. Richardson was lying weltering in his blood, while Mr. King, another member of the party, was severely wounded in the arm. The two unwounded foreigners, accompanied by Mr. King, who with difficulty kept his saddle, were soon flying back to Kanagawa, where Dr. Hepburn, an American medical missionary, attended to the wounded man.

When reports of this attack reached Yokohama, indignation meetings were held, and many residents were anxious to go in a body, overtake the Satsuma procession, and take summary vengeance. It was with difficulty that wiser counsels prevailed. The British minister gave the Yedo government a limited time to deliver up the murderer. But how could the regent order the arrest of a Satsuma samurai, especially while he was with his clan? The time passed, and Satsuma was to receive a lesson. The British fleet proceeded to Kagoshima, Satsuma's chief city, and bombarded it. The Yedo government was then fined five hundred thousand dollars, and Satsuma twenty-five thousand dollars. Both sums were paid, but the murderer escaped arrest.

It was no murder in the eyes of the Satsuma samurai, or in those of any of the other clans, but a necessary act, demanded by the loyalty due to the clan. And when the ugly mood of the men composing Satsuma's escort is taken into consideration, it seems a wonder that any of the party escaped. The government of Yedo was not sorry that Satsuma's pride had been humbled; while the samurai of that clan, known as the bravest of all the brave Japanese samurai, were astounded that they could have been beaten by these foreigners. And they resolved from that time on to master the secret of the barbarian's strength, and to acquire his knowledge. It was the desire to be able to defeat us with our own weapons, combined with the untiring patience of the Japanese character, that led to those changes in Japan which we call its progress, and which so long have seemed inexplicable.

Choshiu, in the meanwhile, continued firing upon vessels passing through the Straits of Shimonoseki, and the ministers of four nations, the United States, England, France, and Holland, made up their minds to punish him. Seventeen men-of-war belonging to those powers attacked Choshiu's forts. The samurai defended themselves bravely, but the Choshiu forts were taken and destroyed. When the clan began negotiations for peace, the two young samurai, Ito and Inouye, returned from England just in time to take an active part in them. They assured their fellow samurai that the fear of an invasion of Japan by a foreign power was baseless. When they were satisfied of this fact, which spread with great rapidity among the two-sworded class, the opposition to foreigners ceased. But the insult to the clan was neither forgiven nor forgotten, and Choshiu, too, decided to dissemble until the samurai had acquired the secret of the barbarians' strength.

Both the Satsuma and Choshiu samurai were now strongly in favor of admitting these foreigners under certain restrictions. They would need them as instructors; they would need also to purchase from them their terrible engines of war. It was now agreed among the ministers of the four powers that the government of Yedo should be given the choice between paying an indemnity of three millions of dollars and opening new ports. It preferred paying the money, and each nation received one fourth, or seven hundred and fifty thousand dollars. The United States afterwards returned its share.

Satsuma and Choshiu were now more than ever determined that the Yedo government must fall, and since all the clans, the Tokugawa and their allies excepted, would rally under the Tennô, they would spare no efforts to get hold of the emperor's person, and to use his authority to form a new government. The regent Iyemochi died in the summer of 1866, and Mito's son, Hitotsubashi Tokugawa (stots' bashee) was appointed to succeed him.

THE TOKUGAWA REGENTS STEP OUT

THE new regent was the last man to uphold the office so long occupied by his ancestors. More of a thinker than a man of deeds, he preferred the quiet of a library to the duties and dangers of power, and it was with reluctance that he accepted the dignity offered him. He would have been well enough pleased, in peaceful times, to hand the responsibilities of his office over to an ambitious prime minister, but these were days when the regent himself must act.

The Tennô in Kyoto seemed to be well disposed toward the new regent, since he gave his sister in marriage to him. But this did not lead to peace. The agitation was more than ever kept up by Satsuma and Choshiu, who had been assured of the help of many powerful clans. Such was the situation when the Tennô, Komei (koh-mi), died, in the beginning of 1867, and the boy Mutsuhito (moots-shtoh), a lad not quite fifteen years old, succeeded to the title and dignity.

Hitotsubashi, or Keiki (kay-kee), the regent, went to Kyoto to pay his respects to the Tennô! How the times had changed in less than a score of years. Twenty years before, the Yedo government was all powerful, and the descendant of the sun goddess was a mere name, a shadow; and now, the eyes of all Japan, and of the foreign ministers also, were fixed upon this boy, the heir to—what? It was more than probable that there would be a change, but one by which only the master or guardian would be affected. For if the idea of a united Japan existed at all, it was only in the minds of a very few men,—Okubo of Satsuma, Kido of Choshiu, and Sanjo and Iwakura the kuge. But the regent saw that his time had come, and on November 9, 1867, he resigned.

This resignation placed the leaders, of the revolution in a quandary. The clans opposed to the Tokugawa were in the majority in the palace, so that now they could use the emperor's authority, but they were perplexed as to what to do. A meeting of the daimio was called for the purpose of deciding the form of the new government, and in the meanwhile the regent was told to continue in his office until further orders. But the daimio did not appear. With the exception of one or two, they were helpless puppets in the hands of their samurai,—men who had never been allowed to originate an idea, or even to decide in matters strictly concerning themselves. And to call a meeting of the leading samurai of the clans would have evoked inter-clannish jealousies, and perhaps a prolonged civil war. It was a dangerous period for Japan.

The foreign ministers had come to Osaka to be present at the opening of that port and of Hiogo, which was to take place on New Year's day, 1868. On the 3rd of January the combined clans seized the palace gates; and the regent, now afraid of personal injury, left Kyoto secretly on the evening of January 6th, and withdrew to the castle of Osaka. The allied clans now summoned him to appear; but, having been advised by the Tokugawa clan to be on his guard, he went, accompanied by about ten thousand samurai, loyal to the Tokugawa house. The allied clans resolved to prevent him from marching upon the capital with his force, and for the third time in the history of Japan the rice fields of Fushimi (foo-shee-mee) saw the fate of Japan decided. The regent was defeated, and fled by sea to Yedo. One of his councilors urged upon him to commit hara-kiri, but Hitotsubashi declined. The man who advised him was honest in the belief that this ought to be done, and, to prove it, committed suicide himself.

The allied clans decided first to subdue those northern clans who still remained faithful to the regent's cause. An army of samurai was easily collected, and, to avoid jealousy, it was commanded in person by the man highest in rank after the Tennô, Prince Arisugawa, while the active command was taken by Japan's ideal samurai, Saigo Takamori of Satsuma. Yedo surrendered after a brief struggle in the temple on the Uyeno (oo-way-noh) heights. But Enomoto (en-noh-moh-toh), the admiral of the regent's fleet, escaped to Hokkaido, taking with him the foreign vessels bought by the regent's government.

The northern clans made the best struggle they could, but the regent was ordered to withdraw to his castle at Shizuoka (sheed-zoo-oh-kah), where he still lives, enjoying himself with experiments in photography. Enomoto first thought of forming a republic in Hokkaido; but the allied clans pursued him, and at last he surrendered, offering to commit hara-kiri if his companions were spared. But the leaders of the new government did not desire to arouse the clan spirit for the sake of revenge; they had one wish: to be able to cope with the foreigners on their own terms, and for that purpose they needed a united Japan. Enomoto and the other Tokugawa leaders were taken into the service of the new government, and were given positions of responsibility according to their ability. Thus Enomoto was minister to Russia, minister of foreign affairs, and, under the last Ito cabinet, minister of commerce and agriculture; while Okubo, who defended Uyeno against the imperial troops, was minister of Japan in Korea at the time the war between China and Japan broke out.

But now the question was: What was the new government to be? The only men able to rule were the samurai, and there were not a few leaders in their own clan who thought that they were the men best fitted for the purpose. Satsuma and Choshiu were prominent on account of the share they had taken in causing the downfall of the Yedo government, and of the samurai of these clans Okubo and Kido were by far the ablest. To avoid jealousy, it was decided that Prince Arisugawa, with the kuge Sanjo and Iwakura, should form the executive, with a board of councilors comprising the most illustrious samurai. This was a wise resolution, for the three men selected ranked head and shoulders above the daimio; so that no clan could feel slighted, whereas the real power remained where it had been for centuries,—in the hands of the best samurai.

The first act of the new government was to ratify the treaties, and from this time the attacks upon foreigners ceased, except in isolated instances. Two of these must be told in detail.

HOW A SAMURAI COMMITTED HARA-KIRI

ON the 4th of February, 1868, the newly opened port of Hiogo, where the foreign settlement Kobe (koh-bay) is located, presented an animated appearance; for the first settlers were unloading their goods, houses were in the course of erection, coolies were shouting, strangers were crowding the streets, and the foreign ministers with their staffs were actively engaged in giving directions or chatting with the less busy members of the young community.

The harbor, too, presented a gay appearance with the many war vessels flying their national flags, and boats passing to and fro. A bright sun showed the glorious blue sky, and there was a general feeling of security, owing to the presence of the fleet and the number of well-armed sailors and marines. Had these been absent, the foreigners would have been very much alarmed. For civil war was raging; troops of armed samurai were constantly moving upon Kyoto, the regent had fled, and no one knew what the morrow might bring forth.

A band of samurai belonging to the Hizen clan were on the march to Kyoto. When they had arrived within the foreign settlement, they were seen to halt; a word of command was given, and then came a whizzing of bullets, fired as fast as repeating rifles could send them forth. Happily these Hizen samurai had not had time to practice sharp-shooting, for most of the bullets went wide of the mark; but had they been good shots, few of the foreigners ashore would have lived to tell the story. The officers of the men-of-war in port heard the firing and suspected the cause. A few orders rang out, boats were manned, and before the Hizen men were quite out of the place, the guards of the different legations, and the soldiers and marines of the war vessels, were after them. But the Hizen samurai, having heard of Shimonoseki and Kagoshima, did not wait for them, so the foreign troops had their trouble for nothing.

The whole affair seemed a farce. Two or three men in the foreign settlement had been slightly wounded, and one old woman was shot in the leg. She belonged to the lowest caste of the Japanese, and by the natives was looked upon with contempt. But the foreign doctor examined her, and had her taken in and made comfortable, notwithstanding the protests of the native servants.

Although the consequences had been slight, the foreign ministers resolved to make an example of the case and insist upon the punishment of the offending officer; and the Tennô's government recognized the justice of the demand. There was no difficulty now about discovering the culprit. Upon receiving the assurance that he would be permitted to commit hara-kiri, the clan delivered him up without raising the slightest disturbance, and the order came under the Tennô seal that delegates from the foreign legations should be allowed to be present to be convinced that the real culprit was brought to justice.

Ito Shunske (ee-to shoons-kay), now Marquis Ito Hirobumi (hee-roh-boo-mee), ex-prime minister of state, the same Choshiu man who had been a house servant in England, was governor of Hiogo. He and another officer were to represent the Tennô at the execution, which was to take place in a temple, the headquarters of the Satsuma men, at half past ten at night. Officers of Satsuma and Choshiu conducted the foreign delegates to the temple, where, after passing through crowds of soldiers standing around camp fires in the temple grounds, they were shown into an inner room.

After they had waited some time, Governor Ito came in, wrote down the names of the foreigners, and told them that seven Japanese officers would witness the execution on behalf of the government. After a short time, the foreigners were invited to enter the hall prepared for the execution. They followed the Japanese witnesses into the main hall, which was lighted by a number of lamps peculiar to Buddhist temples. Before the high altar a cloth of scarlet wool was placed over the mats covering the floor. The Japanese witnesses took their places on the left, the foreigners on the right.

A few minutes passed, and a fine-looking, strongly built man about thirty-two years old, dressed in the state dress of a samurai, walked in quietly, evincing not a sign of emotion. With him came his second, a friend who had undertaken the last service for the condemned man, that of cutting off the head after the deadly incision was made. Three officers wearing the war dress followed. The condemned man first approached the Japanese witnesses, whom he saluted with a stately bow showing no servility,—a salute returned in the same dignified manner. Then, turning to the foreigners, he repeated the salutation. Every one of these foreigners was forced to admire the high-bred demeanor and dauntless courage of this samurai, and all would have been glad to see him pardoned. There was no sign of emotion on the impenetrable countenances of the Japanese spectators.

The man approached the high altar and twice prostrated himself before it. Turning round, he sat down on the scarlet rug, with his second close beside him. One of the three attendants then came forward and brought, upon a tray, the dagger, nine and a half inches long, pointed, and sharp as a razor. Kneeling respectfully before the condemned samurai, the attendant handed him the dagger, and he received it as the Japanese do a valued gift, by raising it to his forehead with both hands; and then he placed it in front of himself.

Again bowing deeply, he prepared to speak. It was expected that he would boast of his deed; for the Japanese samurai, about to die by his own hand, had the right to address the witnesses, and it was customary for him to defend the act that cost him his life by placing it in the best light. But it was evident that this man understood that the unprovoked attack instigated by him might have cost his country dear. It was said afterwards that, before going to his death, he had called his fellow-clansmen, and assured them that the judgment was just, and that no ill will must be shown to those who had brought it upon him. So little does a samurai consider his own welfare when the good of his country is at stake. On this occasion, in a calm and dignified manner he said, with as much hesitation as would be natural in a man making a humiliating confession: "I, and I alone, without cause, gave the order to fire on the foreigners at Kobe, and again as they tried to escape. For this crime I commit hara-kiri, and I beg you who are present to do me the honor of witnessing the act."

After bowing once more, he let his clothes drop to his belt, and took care to tuck the ends of his long sleeves under his knees, so that he should fall forward. Then he took up the dagger, looked at it for a moment almost with affection, and slowly but deeply cut himself. His second jumped up, there was a flash, and the head rolled upon the floor. The two witnesses for the Tennô now crossed over to the foreigners, and called them to witness that justice had been done. They made a suitable answer and departed, deeply moved by the spectacle.

But an example was necessary. The roving samurai had made altogether too free with their swords, and promising lives had been cut short without any provocation. And even this example was not sufficient. It was only when the foreign ministers insisted that all samurai who made an unprovoked attack upon foreigners should be handed over to the executioner and die the death of a common felon, that the attacks ceased. It was the assault on the British minister at Kyoto that led to the enactment of this law.

THE TENNÔ LEAVES HIS SECLUSION

I HAVE told you before that the first act of the new government had been to ratify the treaties, and it was publicly announced that the Tennô had given his consent that foreigners should live in Japan and trade there. The foreign ministers now proposed that they should present their credentials, as the papers appointing them are called, to the Tennô in person, and Okubo and Kido prevailed upon the court to consent that this extraordinary step be taken.

The Heaven Child to be visible! and above all by those foreign intruders who had forced themselves upon the sacred soil of Japan! You may well suppose that the people thought the world was coming to an end, and so far as old Japanese superstitions and the customs of the Middle Ages were concerned, the beginning of the end had certainly come. Kyoto, the sacred city, was to be profaned by the presence of foreigners, who were to be received as welcome guests.

They must be made welcome, for Japan had need of them. Both Okubo and Kido felt sure of it, and although they liked these strangers no better than did the rest of the samurai, they needed them for the advice they could give, the teachers they could supply, and the improvements they could help to introduce. For Japan must be raised from the slough of ignorance into which she had sunk, she must shake off the fetters of useless encumbrances, and must prepare to be able to take her place among the foremost nations of the earth, and lead—not follow. Okubo and Kido knew full well that the path was crooked and thorny, and beset with pitfalls. But if there were no foolish going astray for the purpose of momentary gratification, if the final aim were held constantly in view, greatness would be achieved and no time would be lost.

So the foreign ministers were to be received by this youth of mighty omen! And Kyoto was crowded; for samurai, priests, and idle young men had flocked to the capital, where a new force was opening the era of enlightenment. The British minister was one of the first of western people to stand face to face with the mysterious Heaven Child. He was escorted to the capital as befitted his rank and the dignity of his country; was received and shown to the residence set apart for him during his brief stay; and a Japanese guard of honor watched over his safety.

But two young men, who had come to the old capital, after making merry until they were scarcely able to distinguish right from wrong, began discussing the topics of the day. What subject could be of more absorbing interest than the approaching visit of these bearded foreigners to their Tennô? In maudlin sorrow they began to bewail the disgrace of the country in being compelled to suffer the presence of the strangers, until finally they decided to emulate the rônin, and dispatch some of the unwelcome visitors.

The British minister, unconscious of the plot, at the appointed hour prepared to go to the palace in such state as would impress a people accustomed to set an inordinate value upon pomp and ceremony. The Japanese guard led; then came the mounted escort, followed by the minister and those attached to the legation. Upon turning a corner, there was a commotion, and a man was seen running amuck, and slashing with his sharp sword at the members of the escort. He came, indeed, very near killing the minister. But the Japanese guard was not idle, and before he could work much mischief, the poor, crazed man was severely wounded, taken prisoner, and carried to a neighboring house. This incident prevented the audience from taking place on that day. The Japanese government acted promptly and with energy. A dignified apology was offered to the British minister, who accepted it in the same spirit. The next day the descendant of the sun goddess met the foreigner, and with this meeting began the era of new Japan.

But how were the necessary reforms to be begun?—that was the question facing those who had taken the lead. It was not enough to demolish the structure that had existed since the Middle Ages; it was necessary that the sound timber should be preserved, and used in the more stately building that was to arise upon the ruins of the old. What material must be kept, and what discarded? The first step was taken: the Tennô might remain a god, but he must no longer be a hermit; he must be a ruler in the modern sense of the term; and to perform this task effectually, Kyoto must be left behind, and the seat of government transferred to the capital founded by Iyeyasu, no longer to be called Yedo, but Tokyo, or "eastern capital."

But now a meeting of the nobles was called, to arrange about the next step. The young Tennô, then a lad of sixteen years, attended the meeting, took the oath as ruler, and, instructed by his advisers, promised that "a deliberative assembly should be formed; all measures to be decided by public opinion; the uncivilized customs of former times to be broken through; the impartiality and justice displayed in the workings of nature to be adopted as a basis of action." This promise was afterwards taken to imply a constitutional government.

Acquainted, as we now are, with the Japanese, this proceeding is easily accounted for. The Tennô was speaking, not to the common people, always kept in submission, and satisfied with the usually just and humane rule of the samurai, but to those samurai themselves,—four hundred thousand men, accustomed to be consulted in the management of their clans, and to occupy such offices as their administration rendered necessary. These men, the muscle and brain of the nation, were watching the course of events, and asking, "What is to become of us?" This promise on the part of the government meant, and was understood to mean: "Whatever happens, you shall all have a share in the government under the new order of affairs, and nothing shall be done without consultation with you." The promise had the effect foreseen by the government: the samurai were satisfied to await the course of events.

Okubo, Kido, Goto (goh-toh), and Iwakura were soon convinced that, if the Tennô's government was to acquire real authority, the old feudal system must fall. They consulted with their fellow-clansmen, and persuaded them that their daimio, Satsuma, Choshiu, and Tosa should return their territories to the emperor. The daimio, as you have learned, were only puppets, and when the council of the samurai had decided that it should be so, the lords of the clan could only submit. But Satsuma's samurai, although they consulted, and although the document was sent to the Tennô, reserved to themselves the right to postpone its entering into effect until they were satisfied that their clan would receive due recognition. They were not in favor of a new order of affairs, but preferred a feudal system of which they knew the ways and advantages, to a new system of which they knew nothing, especially if their clan could occupy the position so lately wrested from the Tokugawa.

The plans of Okubo, Kido, and Iwakura, however, met with success. For the other daimio, or rather their samurai, impelled by the example of the great southern clans, also placed their territories in the hands of the Tennô. To accustom the samurai to the change, these lands were now called departments, and the former daimio were appointed as governors.

A new division of the inhabitants was made into the following four classes: 1, the kozoku (koh-dzoh-koo) or imperial princes; 2, the kazoku (kah), the former kuge and the daimio; 3, the shizoku (shee), the former samurai; and 4, the heimin (hi-min), the common people.

Many of the samurai, however, were afraid that too great changes would be harmful to their country. In the deliberative assembly of 1869, the clerk of the house, Ono (oh-noh), introduced a motion proposing to abolish hara-kiri. Only three members out of two hundred and nine spoke in favor of this motion. Six members declined to vote, but two hundred voted against it. In the debate that preceded the voting, the different speakers referred to this peculiar suicide as "the very shrine of the Japanese national spirit, and the embodiment in practice of devotion to principle," "a great ornament to the empire," "a valuable institution, tending to the honor of the nobles, and based on a compassionate feeling toward the official caste," "a pillar of religion and a spur to virtue." And Ono, who introduced this motion, was murdered not long afterwards.

But the leaders of new Japan were determined to control both power and means to carry out the necessary reforms. The income of the former daimio was appropriated by the government, and the old feudal lords received a pension equal to one tenth of their former revenues. But what was to become of the samurai? These men, as a class, despised trade, and were by tradition and education unable to earn their own living. "Give them work that suits them," said Saigo Takamori and those samurai members of the council who sympathized with the fighting qualities of their class. "We have been humiliated by these foreigners, and we are not strong enough to fight them. But there is Korea. It belongs to us, and the king has insulted our Tennô. Let us show these foreigners that, if we are no match for them, we are at least able to vanquish somebody else. And it will please the samurai to show to the world of what stuff they are made."

"It won't do," replied Okubo, Kido, and those men who saw further ahead. "It is true that Korea has refused to receive our embassy and to recognize the Tennô, and we shall settle that little account afterwards. If we did so now, these foreigners might, and probably would, interfere. When we begin that game, we must be able to say: 'Hands off!' and to do so we need an army and a navy such as these foreigners have. We must have experienced officers, able to beat the foreigners at their own game; and, above all, we must provide ourselves with a well-filled purse. No, it will not do at this time."

"But what about the samurai? Are you going to let them starve while you are preparing?" "Well, we shall help them as much as we can, but for the sake of Japan we must employ only the best material; and those samurai who are possessed with the true spirit will not ask for help."

Saigo and the other representatives of the old samurai class resigned their positions, and withdrew in great anger to their former clans. The samurai were granted a pension of twenty dollars a year, or if they wished, they could sell their pensions to the government. The less worthy among them did so. A few became merchants, and I know of some who grew rich. Others spent the money in riotous living, and when it was gone, applied to the government for help, only to receive the answer: "Go and work!" I have known jinrikisha (jin-rik-shah) coolies who had been samurai, but lost caste, and were earning an honest living in this humble manner.

Saigo and his men had the sympathies of a great many samurai, and the government understood that, if it would succeed in its plans, it must have the means to suppress any attempt at rebellion. It was Okubo again who proposed the introduction of a system of conscription by which a number of able-bodied young men of the common people should be compelled to serve in the army. The young samurai of the required age were also admitted into army and navy. French officers were engaged to establish a modern army, and British officers to form a modern navy. Such of the samurai class as gave evidence of ability, were speedily promoted to be officers, and attention was given to the influence of their families in the clan. By these means an effective army, loyal to the Tennô alone, was speedily established.

Schools were opened and instructors were engaged abroad, and the great mass of samurai, too old to learn the new system and discipline of the army, gave ample evidence that they were still the leading power in Japan, by the earnestness with which they applied themselves to the study of foreign languages and books. The efforts of these men were often pathetic,—never ridiculous. They wanted to learn, and they would study indiscriminately any book that came into their hands, with a patience and assiduity that demanded respect.

The same was the case with young samurai boys. Teachers marveled that there was no occasion to keep order. These lads went to school for no other purpose than to learn, and so long as they felt that they were making progress, they were satisfied with their teacher. But woe to the teacher who did not understand his business! The entire class would walk out and simply declare to the authorities that they did not want to study under him. And the discharge of the teacher followed at short notice.

It was natural that the laws and regulations issued by the government should be largely experimental. The aim was simple enough: Japan must be made great and powerful, and this, the real purpose, must be kept hidden from the foreigners. But these experiments, although frequently expensive and annoying, brought experience, which was further increased when a number of influential and sagacious men were sent around the world, to investigate and report upon the laws, customs, and institutions of Europe and America, so that the wheat might be separated from the chaff, and Japan import only such customs and laws as would promote the object in view.

Young men of promise were provided with the means to go abroad for the purpose of acquiring such knowledge as would be of advantage to Japan. You may have met some of these Japanese students. Did you ever know one who was not an earnest worker, who did not accomplish the purpose for which he was sent? Books on all subjects and from all modern languages were translated into Japanese, and eagerly read by these men, who were all actuated by the same impulse: to be able to serve their country.

Foreigners might laugh, and deeply the Japanese samurai felt the insult—for they are acutely sensitive to ridicule—when the government proceeded to order our fashion of dress adopted by the nobles and the official class. The topknot had been sacrificed before this, but the Japanese gentlemen, accustomed to the freedom of movements which the native clothing permits, felt uncomfortable in our close-fitting suits, which rendered them awkward. However, the Tennô himself appeared in public in the uniform of a general, and it was evident that, for the army and navy, at least, our fashion of dress had the advantage. But these experiments, no matter how trivial in themselves, all had the same purpose in view.

SAIGO TAKAMORI

YOU must not suppose that, among the four hundred thousand members of the samurai class, there were not some who disapproved of the acts of the new government. The worthless ones,— and they are to be found among all classes of society,—had indeed been weeded out, but of those who had kept to their caste, although all were impelled by love of their country, there were quite a number who honestly thought that the Tennô's advisers were bringing the country to rack and ruin. Some of the councilors who had resigned were very bitter against their former friends; and several of them, as for instance Eto Shimpei (ay-toh sheem-pay), raised the standard of rebellion. But enough of the clans remained loyal, in those early days, to maintain the authority of the government, and when more serious trouble occurred afterwards, the government was provided with a loyal army and navy, and a single clan could not hope to cope with a united Japan.

Although the most progressive of the Tennô's advisers, Okubo, was a Satsuma man, that powerful and warlike clan was among the most dissatisfied, and the government was afraid to invoke strong measures. When the departments were abolished, and the different provinces were administered by officers sent from Tokyo, and the helpless daimio were ordered to retire into private life as kazoku or nobles, the clan of Satsuma alone was permitted to administer its own affairs. Shimadzu Saburo (shee-mad-zoo sah-boo-roh), the acting and real daimio, had withdrawn in high dudgeon to his seat at Kagoshima, and it required a personal letter from the Tennô, added to the persuasion of a high court noble, Iwakura, to induce him to visit Tokyo.

He protested against everything that he could not understand. "Why cut off the topknot? Why discard the Japanese dress? Why ape these foreigners in everything? Is this the country of the gods or not?" Such were some of the questions asked by him; and although the government offered him high and influential positions, he refused the bait, and sturdily declined to follow the prevailing fashion, but continued to show himself in topknot, Japanese dress, and the inevitable two swords. Staunch old Shimadzu thought that he was representing the samurai class; indeed, he did represent a part of them, and his clansmen deeply sympathized with him, and were intensely loyal.

Among these clansmen, none had more influence than Saigo Takamori. He was the ideal samurai. Of extraordinary height for a Japanese,—he stood over six feet, and the Japanese are of very small stature,—he was of corresponding strength and excelled in all the warlike exercises for which the Satsuma men were famous. He was, besides, very courteous and kind, and withal remarkably brave. You have read how he was banished by the Tokugawa government in the expiring days of the Yedo rule, and how he was made commander in chief of the imperial forces under Prince Arisugawa. He brought the civil war to a close, and was rewarded with a pension for life. This he refused to accept, stating modestly that he had done only his duty; but he was compelled to receive it by special orders from the Tennô himself.

We have seen how, as member of the council, Saigo advised war with Korea. In this he acted on behalf of those samurai who, like himself, too old to learn new methods or to acquire new tactics, were thrown out of all prospect of honorable employment. When he found his advice rejected, he resigned and withdrew to Kagoshima, where, with the pension received from the government, he established and maintained military schools, to which a number of dissatisfied samurai from all parts of Japan flocked. Here they were instructed in the tactics of arms, and especially in the use of that deadly weapon, the old Japanese sword.

The government was, of course, perfectly aware of what was going on, and it was an anxious time when Eto Shimpei revolted. But Saigo remained neutral, and the government began to hope that patriotism would prevail, and that Satsuma would submit at last. Several years passed by, and the railroad to Kyoto was finished in 1878. It had been decided to celebrate this event, and the Tennô himself was to visit the capital of his ancestors, together with the ministers. This programme was carried out. Kyoto was in festive array, and everything was ready, when the news came that Satsuma had raised the standard of rebellion and that Saigo had seized the arsenal at Kagoshima, and was with a large force of samurai on his march through Kiushiu.

The reports were true. To disguise the danger of the situation, the railroad was opened with the appointed ceremonies, but the perturbed ministers decided to make Kyoto the temporary headquarters of the emperor. The government feared what Saigo's advisers had counted upon— that the dissatisfied samurai of other clans would create serious disturbances elsewhere, and it is more than probable that at this time promises and concessions were made, whereby they were assured that henceforward the samurai alone should occupy official positions. But although seriously disturbed, and naturally anxious, the ministers made excellent use of the modern inventions and improvements introduced by them. The telegraph carried orders with lightning speed. Steamships were chartered or purchased, and Saigo's old commander in chief, Prince Arisugawa, was placed in command.

It is very doubtful to me, who knew Saigo well, whether that brave man ever intended to rebel. It is far more probable that his advisers had deceived him into taking up arms. It has, indeed, been proved that a man of humble position was arrested in Kagoshima, who, under torture, was made to confess that he had been sent by the Tennô's ministers to assassinate the Satsuma leader.

Whether Saigo believed this absurd story or not, the other leaders of the clan thought that the moment for action had arrived, and the old samurai spirit of loyalty to the clan impelled Saigo to place himself at its head. Addresses were prepared in which it was stated that the clan did not make war upon the emperor, but upon his advisers, who were ruining the country by the reforms which they had instituted. The imperial arsenal at Kagoshima, in charge of a Satsuma officer, was surrendered to the rebels without a blow, and if they had marched promptly, it is not improbable that Japan would have entered upon a reactionary career.

The island of Kiushiu is very mountainous, and has many difficult passes. The leaders of the imperial army at once decided to surround the revolted province so as to prevent the rebellion from spreading and the insurgents from receiving aid or reënforcement. They succeeded, but only after many hard and desperate battles in which the old samurai spirit showed at its best, and the Japanese sword maintained its old reputation. The government was even compelled to organize a band of swordsmen to cope with the expert Satsuma men.

The clan seemed determined to fight to the death, and despair lent strength to the arms of the samurai, but they could not contend against the organized forces of the government. Kagoshima was taken, and the rebels were hemmed in. But Saigo with a small band of faithful men broke through the circle, recaptured Kagoshima, and fortified himself upon a steep hill beyond the town. Here he defended himself to the last, and when the hill was taken and the leader wounded, a friend performed the last service by cutting off his head. When this gory trophy was brought to the general in command of the imperial forces, he reverently washed it, and had it decently buried. Thousands of samurai visit every year the tomb of one who, although he died a rebel, is considered the last of the old samurai of Old Japan.

JAPAN'S PROGRESS

THE rebellion was subdued, but at great expense. Fifty thousand valuable lives had been lost, and more than five hundred millions of dollars had been spent before this dangerous revolt was stamped out. And what had been taught by it? Two lessons which the government must take to heart. The first was that the samurai, as a class, must remain the rulers of Japan, and the next was that such national customs as did not interfere with the progress and future greatness of their country, must not only be left untouched, but be fostered and encouraged.

Okubo, who, by his energy, had conduced not a little to the defeat of Satsuma, was considered a traitor to his clan, and no one was astonished when he was attacked in his carriage in Tokyo, and assassinated, although many mourned his loss. This murder proved how desperate was the samurai spirit, and from this time all the offices were filled by members of this class, while a reaction commenced, under their leadership, tending toward the preservation of Japanese laws, habits, and customs, without hindrance to the improvement of army and navy, the building of railroads, and the developing of the resources of the country.

The kuge members of the cabinet or council had died or retired, and the government was actually in the possession of the samurai. But the most prominent of these who were not actually members of the cabinet, clamored for more influence. I have shown you the numerous good qualities of the samurai: the love for their country, their courage, and unselfishness. But while these characteristics are common to them, they have also another which is equally conspicuous, and that is conceit. A great many of them believe that they, and they alone, are able to rule the country; and each one is impatient because he is not at once appointed prime minister.

Several newspapers had been established in Tokyo and elsewhere, and the samurai, who soon recognized the influence of public opinion, took good care that these papers came under their control. They now could, and did, clamor openly for more influence. "Why don't you establish a parliament, and give us a constitution?" they asked. "His Majesty the Tennô"—mentioning the emperor with expressions of the greatest reverence—"was good enough to promise us this boon. It is you, the emperor's advisers, who prevent him. You are traitors to him and to your country."

The ministers could, and did, suspend such papers, but others sprang up and repeated the complaint over and over again. The ministers had the good sense not to be too sensitive to these remarks, and to decline handing the government over to these self-constituted critics. But a number of the samurai began at last to believe that they had a real grievance, and the government was compelled in 1880 to promise that a constitution would be given and a parliament established within ten years from that time. The clamoring samurai had to be satisfied with this, but there were other ways in which to keep themselves prominently before their fellow-clansmen, and one of these was by the agitation of revision of the treaties.

I have told you several times that the samurai rule the people of Japan in a just and humane manner, but in return they expect the deepest reverence and implicit obedience. Now when the first treaties were made, very little was known of the Japanese by foreigners. But the ministers of foreign nations did know that they had no written laws, that torture could be applied at the option of the judge, and that a certain number of blows was a mild and moderate punishment. Under these circumstances they refused, of course, to allow their fellow-citizens to be brought before native judges, and it was stated in the treaties that foreigners should be judged only according to their own laws and before the consuls appointed by their government.

These treaties should have been revised in 1872; but although the Japanese had been at work to establish a code of written laws, the foreign ministers were not satisfied that their fellow-citizens would obtain justice, and the revision of the treaties was constantly postponed. This roused the Japanese samurai to anger. "Why may we not judge those proud, arrogant foreign merchants, who imagine themselves as good if not better than a samurai?"

The government, although it appeared to exert itself to the utmost, was not in reality anxious to have jurisdiction over foreigners. It knew that in a case of a foreigner against a samurai, not a judge in Japan (where every judge belongs to the samurai class) would dare give a judgment in favor of the foreigner, and it knew also that foreign governments were in the habit of seeing their subjects protected in their rights. But the samurai as a class did not take this point of view. They wanted to be able to humble those proud foreigners, and to avenge themselves for the slights to which some of them had been exposed.

Count Okuma (oh'-koo-mah), then prime minister, had a dynamite bomb thrown under him, which wounded him so severely as to render amputation of a leg necessary.

These events show how much of our civilization had been acquired by the Japanese. Count Ito went to Europe to study the different constitutions, and when he returned he prepared one after the law of the German Empire. Japan was to have a Diet, as the German Congress is called, consisting of two houses, as does our own Congress. The House of Representatives was to be elected by the people, but the samurai would take good care that none but members of their class should take a seat. This was not very difficult, for the people were really well pleased to attend to their own business and leave the duty of governing, that is, of making laws and executing them, to their old-time masters who had nothing else to do, and plenty of experience besides. The House of Lords, corresponding to our Senate, consisted of hereditary members such as princes of the blood; that is, princes related to the emperor and the highest kuge and daimio.

The other nobles were elected by members of their own rank; but the emperor had the right to appoint members for special services. This and the fact that several samurai had received titles equal to or even higher than their former lords, rendered it highly probable that the nobles would vote as the samurai decided. But to make this still more certain, they appointed members of their own class as stewards in the residences of the kuge, daimio, and even of the imperial princes, who were to receive the salaries, pensions, or revenues of these nobles, and disburse them. They found cause for doing so in the fact that some nobles, unaccustomed to think or act for themselves, and never having been allowed to spend money, were found, upon receiving a more or less large sum, to commit extravagances promising speedy impoverishment. The nobles did not object any more than the common people; and so these samurai could influence, if not control, the votes of their employers.

The promised constitution was duly published in 1889; the Tennô took the oath to his divine ancestors, and the Diet was opened with great festivities. The Houses met, and, for novices in parliamentary debate, did very well. Of course, the heat of discussion would sometimes lead to breaches of that politeness for which the Japanese samurai are celebrated; but the odd spectacle was offered of an overwhelming majority in the opposition without its members being able to agree among themselves. This was owing to the humble opinion hidden in each breast that the owner was the only man for the occasion, and that he, for the glory of Japan, should at once be appointed prime minister.

The members of the cabinet were constantly attacked in the debate. For a long time the revision of the treaties was the apparent cause. But England signed the revised treaty in 1894; other nations did the same; and foreigners living in Japan will be placed under Japanese jurisdiction when the new treaties go into effect, that is, on July 16, 1899.

WAR WITH CHINA

IT was twenty-six years since 1868, when Japan's leading samurai had formed the plan to introduce reforms which would enable the Tennô's realm to hold its own among the civilized nations of the earth. Had success crowned their efforts? Was this country indeed able to brave any of the powers that had humiliated it at Kagoshima and Shimonoseki? Had the longed-for time at last arrived when deeply resented insults could be wiped out and old scores paid off?

You have seen how the refusal of Korea to receive the Tennô's ambassador had been resented by the more impatient samurai, and how the unwillingness of the government to take speedy revenge had led to serious revolts. A few years later, another effort had been made to enter into communication with the king of Korea, and again an insult had been offered. These slights, apparently passed over, had not been forgotten; and when, in 1876, the Japanese had the opportunity to dispatch an armed force without alarming either Russia or England, they compelled the Koreans to enter into a treaty of friendship and commerce, and obtained the right to reside and trade in three seaports and in the capital, Soül

In the opinion of the Japanese samurai, Korea was a dependency of Japan, owing to the conquest first under Empress Jingu and afterwards under the regent Hideyoshi; and it was therefore no wonder that the Japanese minister in Korea used his utmost endeavors to bring that peninsula under the rule of the Tennô. Serious disturbances took place twice, and the cause was easily traceable to Japanese intrigues. It was to counteract them that Li Hung Chang, the great Chinese statesman, advised the Korean king to enter into treaties with other nations; so that in 1882 Commodore Shufeldt signed a treaty on behalf of the United States, and since that time Americans may reside and trade in that unhappy Land of the Morning Calm. England, France, Germany, and Russia made treaties similar to that with the United States.

In 1884 a serious disturbance took place. The Japanese had made an agreement with a high Korean official, Kim ok Kyun (kyoon), to capture and carry off the king; but the plot failed, and both the Japanese minister and the Korean, with his fellow-conspirators, fled to Japan. After that Kim ok Kyun lived in Japan, where he was supported for ten years by the Japanese. In March, 1894, he was induced to come to Shanghai, where he was murdered by a Korean. The honor paid by China and Korea to the murderer made the Japanese furious.

It must be stated here that there is no country on earth, not even China, that is so wretchedly governed as Korea. The officers seem to be appointed for the sole purpose of robbing and stealing. A Korean farmer, when his crop of rice is very bountiful, will harvest only enough to support him and his family until the next season, and to have sufficient for seed. "Why should I harvest more?" a Korean will say, "that the mandarins (officers) may come and rob me of it? If they want that rice, let them go and cut it themselves."

There had been a failure of the crop in a southern province of Korea, and several people, dissatisfied with the officers, had begun a small rebellion. These people called themselves reformers, and they robbed and plundered until the king sent some soldiers against them. But these soldiers accomplished nothing, and the rebels did as they pleased.

The foreign ministers in Korea, with the exception of Mr. J. N. B. Sill, minister of the United States, Otori, minister of Japan, and Yuan (yoo-ahn), minister of China, were all absent on their vacation, when Yuan insisted that the king should ask the emperor of China for help to subdue the rebels. The king resisted for three weeks, but when the queen and her cousin Min, the prime minister, also begged him to do so, he submitted, and the request was sent. The Japanese kept themselves well informed, and the fact was soon known to the Tokyo government.

Japan had entered into a treaty with China, by which each agreed to send no troops into Korea without notifying the other power; and when Japan knew that China was preparing to dispatch a force, it was decided that now or never was the time to try the efficiency of army and navy, and at the same time to satisfy the war party of the samurai, and incidentally to settle old scores with Korea. No better time could have been chosen. Neither Europe nor America expected any disturbance, and no single power was prepared to interfere, while jealousy prevented the great powers of Europe from acting together. When at last China was ready to send troops, and notified Japan, the Japanese minister in Peking made a similar communication to the Chinese government. And so much dispatch had been used by the Japanese authorities that Otori (oh'-toh-ree) could boast that the Japanese troops had landed at the port of Soul one hour before the first Chinese soldiers came ashore.

And now the Japanese government, knowing that the die was cast, continued its preparations steadily, but as secretly as possible. The reserves of the army were called out, and the navy left for Korea, every man determined to do his duty. The Japanese then gave notice to the Chinese government not to send any more troops; declaring that if it did so, the government would consider it an unfriendly act, in other words, it would mean war.

The Chinese government had engaged several English vessels to transport Chinese soldiers, and one of these, an English ship, the Kowshing, was overtaken by a Japanese man-of-war, and ordered to follow her. The captain signaled that the Chinese prevented him from obeying, whereupon he was advised to jump over-board. The Japanese now fired upon the transport, and sunk her.

This happened in July, 1894. The Japanese, in the meanwhile, had continued sending troops to Korea, until there were about three thousand men in Soül, while the Chinese had fortified themselves at Asan (ah-sahn), a port on the western coast of Korea. It was decided to drive out the Chinese troops, and Otori demanded of the king that he should order them to leave. The king replied mildly that he could not very well do so, since they had been sent at his request. But Otori knew how the Koreans detested the Japanese, so he decided to capture the king and keep him as a hostage, while the Japanese army left for the south.

At four o'clock of the morning of July 23, 1894, the Japanese minister took the necessary measures. The city walls, near the palace, were occupied by his troops, and a detachment marched to the principal gate of the palace. They first attempted to burn the gate, but when this failed, they scaled the wall with a ladder and opened the gate from the inside. They then entered the grounds and marched upon the palace. Here was the frightened Korean guard, and a shot was fired. Who fired it will probably never be known, but an engagement followed in which one Japanese and seventeen Koreans were killed, and several of each party were hurt. The Japanese occupied the palace and kept the king a prisoner in it.

They were now ready to march upon Asan, and lost no time in doing so. Have you, my young friends, any idea of what a Chinese army is? Try, if you can, to imagine soldiers going to war with umbrellas, to keep from getting wet if it should rain! And think of officers who have studied tactics that say: "When you are in the presence of the enemy, put on hideous masks, and make horrible noises, so that they may be frightened." I have seen Chinese soldiers going to fight the Japanese, armed with bamboo poles, sharpened with tenpenny nails at the top. And I have seen others who when ready to fire off their guns, would close their eyes, and pull the trigger. These men were not regular soldiers at all; they were coolies, hired for this war. Most of them were stalwart enough, and with plenty of drill, they could have been trained as soldiers; untrained as they were, and led by cowardly and ignorant officers, what chance had they against the well-disciplined, drilled, and splendidly commanded troops of Japan—a nation naturally warlike?

The Japanese troops had come to fight, and went into battle willing to die for their Tennô and their country. The Chinese had been promised fifty taels (about $37.50) for every Japanese head they brought to their general. So they wanted to cut off heads, but did not care about losing their own. In the battle near Asan, on July 29, 1894, the Japanese utterly routed the enemy. The Chinese dispersed; the officers and generals disguised themselves as coolies, and made their way north.

China had sent reënforcements, and its troops then occupied a very strong position at Ping-yang, on the Tatung River. August passed by without further fighting, although war had been regularly declared on the first of that month. On the 14th of September, the Japanese army, in command of Field Marshal Yamagata (yah-mahng'-ah-tah), was opposite the enemy, and on the 15th and 16th a battle took place. The Manchurian cavalry, a body of five hundred men, made a charge, but that was all the fighting, so far as the Chinese were concerned. The Japanese took a steep hill at the point of the bayonet, and easily dislodged the Chinese. Ping-yang was taken, and Yamagata began his march north to the Yalu (yah-loo) River, which forms the boundary between China and Korea.

This part of China is called Manchuria, and is the cradle of the present house of Chinese emperors. They were very sorry to see this province invaded, and prepared to send strong reënforcements to arrest the Japanese march. This led to the first and only naval battle of the war. While the Japanese fleet was scouring the Yellow Sea to intercept the enemy's transports, smoke was seen in the distance to the north. Steaming in that direction, Admiral Ito, in command of the Japanese fleet, discovered that it was the famous North China fleet, and that it had been conveying transports.

The eager Japanese at once prepared for battle, and since their fleet hemmed the enemy in on the sea side, the Chinese were compelled to engage in a fight for which they had but little taste. They had, in reality, a stronger force than the Japanese, and their two battle-ships alone, the Ting-yuen (teng-yoon) and the Chengyuen (cheng-yoon), ought to have defeated the less powerful Japanese fleet. But the weakness of the Tennô's vessels was more than counterbalanced by the patriotism, courage, and seamanship of the officers and crew. Every man, from admiral to powder monkey, was eager for the fight, and firmly resolved to do his duty. The result was easy to foretell. The Chinese lost several vessels, and it was with difficulty that the pride of China's navy, the two battleships from which such great things had been expected, made their way back to Wei-hai-wei (way-hi-way). This battle made the Japanese masters of the Yellow Sea, and the great Chinese empire could send no more troops by water.

Yamagata had little difficulty in forcing his way across the Yalu River, and started upon his long march to Peking. At this time, that is, in the beginning of November, a second army had left Japan, and, without meeting any obstruction, had landed at Ta-lien-wan (tah-lyen-wahng), a sheltered bay on the southeast coast of the Liao-tung (lee-ah-oh-tongue) peninsula.

If you will take the map of Japan, and look at that large gulf called the Yellow Sea, you will see a smaller body of water, the Gulf of Pechili (pech-ee-lee), to the northwest of it. This is the key to Peking, the capital of China. On the north, this entrance was protected by the southern point of the Liao-tung peninsula, known as Port Arthur. The ablest engineers had constructed the walls and forts, and the natural position was so strong that foreign military men had pronounced it impregnable.

Right opposite the Liao-tung peninsula, on the southern coast of the Gulf of Pechili, is the Shan-tung (shahn-tongue) peninsula. West of its northeastern extremity is a small natural harbor, defended by steep islands in front. Here, too, the hand of man has aided the forces of nature, and the result is a basin where, with the most ordinary precautions, a fleet may remain in complete security, and mock at the efforts of the boldest enemy.

Japan had firmly decided to march upon Peking and to dictate there the terms of peace to the "Solitary Man," as the Chinese call their emperor. But to prevent being attacked in the rear, she wanted to capture both Port Arthur and Wei-hai-wei. As she could not hope to be able to take Port Arthur by a front attack, she concluded to approach it from the land side, that is, from the rear. That is why Marshal Oyama (oh-yahmah) had landed at Ta-lien-wan, and was now on the march against the strong fortress.

Escape by way of land was cut off to the Chinese braves (as the soldiers were called) defending the fortress, and the presence of the Japanese fleet prevented their escape by sea. Now, driven in a corner, even Chinese soldiers will fight. But what could they do against the well-drilled and disciplined troops of Japan? The officers commanding the Tennô's troops were old Satsuma or

Choshiu samurai, who were now in their true element. Field Marshal Oyama was in supreme command, and General Yamaji (yah-mah-yee), the Blind Dragon, as he was affectionately called by his troops, because he had but one eye, commanded the attack. Yamaji gained much honor by his coolness and supreme indifference to danger. On November 21, the impregnable stronghold was captured, and the red sun on the white field floated over China's strongest fortress.

Up to this time the Japanese had conducted the war most humanely, and had earned the well-deserved admiration of the whole civilized world. The discipline had been perfect. No blood had been shed wantonly; peaceful inhabitants had been left undisturbed in life and property, and prisoners taken in battle had been kindly cared for. The wounded Chinese had received the same care and attention as was given to the wounded Japanese, and the severest critic could find no cause for reproach.

How differently had the Chinese acted! Wounded Japanese on a battlefield were eagerly sought, that they might be robbed of their clothing and valuables, and their heads were cut off for the sake of the promised reward. The cool and brave members of the Red Cross Society, when searching for the wounded, regardless whether they were friends or enemies, had been frequently attacked by these Chinese monsters, and when taken prisoners had been mutilated and put to death. A brave foreign naval officer, who was not in sympathy with Japan, told me that if American or European soldiers had conducted this war, they would have laid waste the territory through which they passed, to teach the Chinese the lesson that such barbarous cruelty can not remain unpunished.

When the Japanese entered Port Arthur and witnessed there the horrible outrages committed upon their countrymen, they were filled with rage, and determined to retaliate. The whole population was put to the sword, the innocent suffering with the guilty; but the Chinese for once received a much-needed lesson.

Through the inclement climate of Manchuria, in a desert of snow and ice, the first army corps continued slowly to advance. There was some doubt whether they would proceed to the northeast and capture Moukden (monk-den), the capital of Manchuria, or continue their way toward the Chinese capital.

It was in the latter part of January, 1895, that the third army, placed in command of Field Marshal Oyama, left for the Shan-tung peninsula to capture Wei-hai-wei in conjunction with the fleet. Again the army landed without difficulty, some distance east of the doomed stronghold, and, dividing into three corps, advanced by rapid marches. The Chinese had sunk several junks, and further strengthened the defenses of the entrance to the basin containing their crippled fleet, by a strong chain. But little did the bold Japanese care. Torpedo boats succeeded in effecting an entrance, and one of them rammed one of the great battleships so that she sunk at her moorings. Fleet and fortress surrendered, and the Chinese admiral, knowing that he would be held responsible for the loss of the fleet, committed suicide. At last Niuchwang (nee-oo-chwang) was reached and taken May 4.

Meanwhile China had grown tired of the war. The Japanese had exposed the incapacity and corruption of the Chinese government, and no foreign power showed any desire to come to its rescue. The Japanese were, naturally enough, elated over their victories, and the native press began to suggest that it was time to establish a protectorate over the huge empire, and that the Japanese were the people to assume that duty. The Chinese began to express a wish to enter into negotiations for peace. But the Japanese declined receiving any one who was not provided with full authority to sign a treaty, and in the meanwhile continued their preparations to send a third army.

The emperor had established his headquarters at Hiroshima (hee-ro-shee-mah), and had called a session of the Diet, to vote the necessary money to carry on the war. There was, of course, no opposition. Every member, every samurai, would gladly have given his last penny and his life, had the glory of Japan demanded it. Even the people had taken the patriotic fever, and poor jinrikisha coolies would devote part of their scanty earnings to increase the war fund composed of voluntary contributions.

China's old statesman, Li Hung Chang, was now called to Peking, and ordered to proceed to Japan, to make peace. Before leaving, he called on the foreign ministers and probably satisfied himself as to how much the Japanese would be allowed to demand. Through the United States minister in Tokyo, the Japanese government was informed of Li's arrival, and Shimonoseki, Japan, was appointed as the place where the negotiations should be held. The Chinese government had engaged the services of Hon. John W. Foster of Washington, D.C., on account of his knowledge of international law.

Li Hung Chang arrived in Japan and met our old friend, Ito, the prime minister, who was appointed by the Tennô to represent Japan. One day, as the Chinese minister was returning from the meeting, a young Japanese fired a small revolver at him. The bullet penetrated above the eye.

The murderer was taken prisoner, and upon examination it was found that he was not a samurai, but the son of a poor farmer, who had shown a worthless character from early youth. He had joined the soshi (soh-shee),—young vagabonds, too lazy to work, who openly sell their services to the highest bidder, to produce a riot, to commit murder, or any other lawless act. They are known to the government and to the police, and not only are they tolerated, but it seems they even receive support. The only explanation that can be given is that their leaders are samurai, which would fully account for their immunity. The murderer was arraigned in court, and condemned to imprisonment for life.

His victim recovered, and the peace negotiations were resumed. At last the two statesmen came to an agreement. By the terms of the treaty of Shimonoseki, signed on April 17, 1895, the independence of Korea was to be acknowledged, China was to give to Japan the island of Formosa, the Liao-tung peninsula, and other territory, besides paying an indemnity of two hundred million taels (about one hundred and forty-eight million dollars); so you see that her incapacity and corruption cost her very dear. But now Russia, France, and Germany interfered. The ministers of those countries gave Japan the friendly advice not to take the Liao-tung peninsula, which meant the same thing as saying: "You shall not do it!" The Japanese government understood it in that way; and knowing that it could not hope to fight those three countries with any chance of success, it submitted, agreeing to accept, instead, an additional indemnity of thirty million taels.

You can easily understand how angry the Japanese, and especially the samurai, were when they heard of this interference. But they could do nothing but disguise their feelings, and continue their preparations until at last they might be able to retaliate on all the nations that had thwarted or insulted them.

MUTSUHITO, EMPEROR OF JAPAN

ON November 3, 1852, while Commodore Perry was making preparations to sail for Japan, the present emperor, Mutsuhito, was born, in the old Tennô palace in Kyoto. His father, Emperor Komei, had lived, as had the descendants of the sun goddess for so many hundreds of years, in absolute seclusion from the world, seeing only the faces of the members of his immediate household, who prostrated themselves in the dust whenever they approached their august sovereign. Within the palace he reigned supreme; and it is more than probable that he imagined that his will was law throughout the empire. But the regents were masters of Japan, and at the time of Mutsuhito's birth there seemed very little likelihood that the heir to the throne would be more than a shadow ruler.

He was taught to read and write Chinese as well as Japanese characters; to reverence the gods, his ancestors, and above all, his father, as their living representative; he learned, from earliest youth, to behave himself with the dignity due to his birth, and to act upon the suggestions of such of his attendants as by birth and rank were entitled to offer them.

He had absolutely no amusements. He did not know what the words "playmate" and "toy" meant. To the Japanese boy, from samurai up to Tennô, there exists no such thing as play or fun. Life to him is a sober existence revolving around one center,—duty.

The seeds of revolution planted during the two hundred and fifty years of peace under the descendants of Iyeyasu had begun to sprout. Perry's arrival acted like a warm rain after a prolonged drought, and signs appeared everywhere that the harvest was at hand. Did those hermits within the palace walls note the signs of the times, or were they too august to be informed that their dwelling was guarded more jealously than ever, that armed samurai, trusted councilors of powerful clans, were hiding in the old capital, and that the Yamato Damashii was abroad, looking toward the descendant of the gods, and imploring help from him?

I do not think it likely that Emperor Komei knew anything of what was going on; but in all probability the boy Mutsuhito was kept pretty well informed. His attendants, while he was still heir apparent, could and would talk before him, and the lessons thus gained were a good preparation for his future career.

We have seen that Emperor Komei died early in 1867, and the boy, not yet fifteen years old, ascended the throne amid the struggles of a civil war. His actions were, of course, determined upon by the kuge in conjunction with the leading samurai of the allied clans. This council communicated its decisions to the imperial princes or miya, who, in their turn, imparted them to the Tennô. Thus, it was decided that he should personally receive the foreign ministers, that he should marry the present empress, a daughter of the house of Ichijo (ee-chee-joh), and that he should leave Kyoto and take up his residence in Yedo, thereafter to be called Tokyo, or eastern capital.

From his education, the boy emperor had acquired two valuable qualities: obedience to the suggestions of trusty councilors, and that quiet submission to duty which is the foundation of character in any boy.

He was the first of his race—since more than a thousand years ago his ancestors had withdrawn from active life—to show himself freely to his people. He discarded in public the old national dress, and in his official life conforms to the customs and manners of a foreign court, although within the privacy of his own apartments, he prefers the dress and food of his youth.

But what an era does his reign present to his people! Well may it be called Meiji (may-jee), Enlightened Progress. Under his reign the palpable differences of caste have disappeared. No more daimio or kuge with their mediæval privileges! No more attacks on harmless merchants by playful samurai bent upon testing the metal of their swords. No more eta (ay-tah), outcasts of society, but equality of all before the law, with a slight reservation in favor of the samurai, or "official class"!

And with these changes, wealth and prosperity have come to the people. The intercourse with other nations has brought new industries. When the Tennô first entered Yedo, he spent twelve days on the fatiguing journey from the old imperial city. Now the iron horse brings him there in less than twenty-four hours. More than three thousand miles of railroad have been built with Japanese capital and enterprise, and as many more are in the course of construction. The telegraph conveys the emperor's commands to the farthest corner of his empire; telephone and electric lights testify to Japan's ability to appreciate the inventions of this age.

Factories have been built and furnish labor to tens of thousands of workmen, while wages have risen and savings increase. And Japan's army and navy, too,—her greatest pride—have kept pace with the progress of the times, and have compelled respect from abroad. Japan has taken her place as one of the great powers of the earth. Her flag begins to be known on the seas. Her merchant vessels are seen in Europe, Australia, and on the coast of America, as well as in the eastern parts of the Pacific. Her scholars compete with those of western universities.

Western civilization hails Japan's advent. Mutsuhito and his empire have gained the admiration and respect of the world, and the world acknowledges the high qualities of the ruling class, the samurai or shizoku. They will be regarded with suspicion unless they forego their scheme of revenge, and decide to enhance the glory of their country and its Tennô by other means than a career of conquest. But for what they have accomplished thus far, American boys and girls will heartily join those of Japan in shouting: "Nippon Ban-zai! (nee-pon ban-zi) Long live Japan!

www.ingramcontent.com/pod-product-compliance
Lightning Source LLC
Chambersburg PA
CBHW020842160426
43192CB00007B/756